T0117122

When the

Lily Blooms

When the Lily Blooms

Reflections to Restore the Heart and Soul

Jayne Kane

iUniverse, Inc.
Bloomington

When the Lily Blooms
Reflections to Restore the Heart and Soul

Copyright © 2012 by Jayne E. Kane.

All rights reserved. No part of this book may be used or reproduced by any means, graphic, electronic, or mechanical, including photocopying, recording, taping or by any information storage retrieval system without the written permission of the publisher except in the case of brief quotations embodied in critical articles and reviews.

iUniverse books may be ordered through booksellers or by contacting:

iUniverse
1663 Liberty Drive
Bloomington, IN 47403
www.iuniverse.com
1-800-Authors (1-800-288-4677)

Because of the dynamic nature of the Internet, any web addresses or links contained in this book may have changed since publication and may no longer be valid. The views expressed in this work are solely those of the author and do not necessarily reflect the views of the publisher, and the publisher hereby disclaims any responsibility for them.

Any people depicted in stock imagery provided by Thinkstock are models, and such images are being used for illustrative purposes only.
Certain stock imagery © Thinkstock.

ISBN: 978-1-4759-1040-7 (sc)
ISBN: 978-1-4759-1042-1 (hc)
ISBN: 978-1-4759-1041-4 (ebk)

Printed in the United States of America

iUniverse rev. date: 05/22/2012

All Scripture quotations, unless otherwise indicated, are taken from the Holy Bible: New International Version ®, NIV®, 1973, 1978, 1984, 2008 by International Bible Society. Used by permission of Zondervan. All rights reserved worldwide. www.zondervan.com

The "NIV" and "New International Version" are trademarks registered in the United States Patent and Trademark Office of Biblica, Inc ™

Contents

SILENCE

SURRENDER

Acknowledgments

I could not have had the healing and restoration in my life I did without the help of numerous individual and ministries who came along side me during the journey. I am so grateful to them. My first thanks goes to God, my father, my friend, my partner, my gardener and my restorer. I love that He would love me so much that He would put up with me, stay with me and never abandon me, even when I was being *impossible.*

Pacem In Terris, St. Francis, Minnesota
Ministry of Reconciliation; Marlis Kulus and Carolyn Singer
Healing the Heart of the Family; Jack and Trisha Frost
Help for the Helpers, Minneapolis, MN
Freedom in Christ Ministries; Neil Anderson
Alpha ®
Life Purpose Coaching Centers International ®; Dr. Katie Brazelton
Crown College, St. Bonifacius, Minnesota
Students Today Leaders Forever, Minneapolis, Minnesota
Hosanna Lutheran Church, Lakeville, Minnesota
Sozo Healing Ministry; Dawna DeSilva
West Union Lutheran Church, Carver, Minnesota
Valley Evangelical Free Church, Chaska, Minnesota

I would also like to thank the following people for helping me with this project:
Amy Kay Anderson, for prayerfully and generously doing the cover design
Amadeline Baird, for editing and proofing my work
Deb Stuewe; my life long friend and prayer partner
Pastor Mike and Sandy Sindelar, Valley Evangelical Free Church, Chaska, Minnesota
Patty Robinson; my life coach

Penny Bertsch; my life plan facilitator
Dori Finch; my employer, mentor and encourager
Larry Zellmann, who continues to carry on the Truths of God that my dear friend, Lois, clung to during her time here on earth.
And of course Tim and Tony, my sons, my joy and my reason for wanting to leave a legacy.

Introduction

As a little girl I was drawn to the pasture that sprawled behind the grove of trees on my parent's farm. In the spring time the low area of this pasture filled with water. I loved wading through it, hoping it wouldn't get so deep it would pour over the top of my boots and I would end up with wet socks. Many times I would take a walking stick with me, which was usually a tree branch stripped of its leaves. This would be my measuring stick to check the depth of the water and my aid if I got stuck in the mud. I always went to the pasture alone and as I walked, I would sing *Jesus Loves Me.* I would marvel at God's creation: geese flying overhead, leaves sprouting on the trees, frogs jumping to get out of the way, and various flowers and weeds of which I had no idea what the names were.

It seemed as though the times I needed to go to the pasture were when I was sad. I was small for my age and teased for this in school. Living on a farm there was never a lack of things to keep busy with, but I didn't have easy access to friends. So I struggled with loneliness and feelings of inadequacy and insignificance. But even at a young age I found peace and security and perhaps a subconscious presence of the Lord on those walks. Those times are some of my favorite childhood memories.

My time in the pasture each spring was limited, as the grass turned green and the temporary pond dried up. When this happened it was time for the cows to take over. I was afraid of them and somehow the simplicity, silence, solitude and place to surrender in the pasture became a haven for the cows. Nevertheless, I had experienced something that would be vital to me in the years to come.

As I allowed my imagination to run wild on these adventures in the pasture, I would envision my future as a grown up. I would meet a man, fall in love and have a beautiful home with flowers and trees all around it. I would be a teacher or a nurse (if I didn't have to give shots) or in some kind of a profession like it, where people could learn, would get better and could grow and be healed.

Another thing I did in the pasture was I would imagine what the past had been like out there. My great-great grandfather homesteaded the farm, cleared woods and established this corner of the earth for generations to come. It is how he left a legacy. I pictured the woods that had once been there, the hardwood trees such as oak and maple. I imagined rocks scattered throughout the woods to sit on, and pockets of water, small ponds and springs that provided water for the wildlife. These creatures had since left to find habitat in other places not being farmed.

As I walked along I would take my walking stick and make little streams and waterways in the mud of the flooded low area. I would try to make them flow naturally and take the rocks from the rock pile my dad made and form them into little sitting places where I could rest. My dad loved horticulture and he would buy seedling trees and I would help him plant these in the pasture in hopes of one day restoring the land for wildlife and nature.

Recently I drove by the farm where I grew up. It was sold when my parents died and a new house was built on the edge of the pasture. On the spring day I drove by, the low area of the pasture was flooded. The trees that Dad and I planted have grown up and matured, but most of the trees from the virgin woods are gone. The pasture is still the same in many ways, yet different. The pasture was a place to go to be away from the problems of childhood. It was my sanctuary and a place where I could be restored. This place sang to the core of my being and even as a little girl God knew his plan for me. In fact, before I was born, way back when great-great grandfather was settling the land, God knew me and was setting me apart for his plan (Jeremiah 1:5). God knew being a restorer would be my driving passion. As I made those little ponds and planted little seedling trees in the sanctuary of the pasture, God was planting seeds in me.

Those times of finding simplicity, silence, solitude and surrender in the pasture have become pivotal elements in God's restoration of me to him. As you spend time in this book restoring your body, mind and spirit, it is my prayer that the love of Jesus, the truth of God's Word and the work of the Holy Spirit will work a miracle of restoration in you. My passion is to see people restored and blooming, just as the new blooms of spring happen every year. As you will discover, it is God's desire for you too.

As you begin this book, take the childhood song I would sing in the pasture, and read it. If you don't believe these words or have a difficult time even getting through it, this is what God's restoration is all about. It is the starting point for you.

So be encouraged! No matter what the circumstances of your life have been there is hope and help for you. Enjoy the journey with me as you read on.

Jesus loves me! This I know,
For the Bible tells me so;
Little ones to him belong,
They are weak, but he is strong.
Yes Jesus loves me! Yes, Jesus loves me!
Yes, Jesus loves me! The Bible tells me so.
By Anna B. Warner
1820-1915
Public Domain

About This Book

This book is being written with the intent that the promises of God will restore you in every way imaginable. It is our human nature to wish for instantaneous results, but as I discovered God has no limits on time and he is a God of refinement (Zechariah 13:9). I would encourage you to take this book and use it in whatever way would be most beneficial. It is written with the intent that it would be multifaceted and can be used in a variety of ways. For me, it is personal, visual and transparent. I want my readers to know we all face basically the same struggles. On the other side of the struggle we can all be healed, restored and be overcomers.

When the Lily Blooms is divided into four sections. During a time of searching when I was in the wilderness God gave me four words; simplicity, solitude, silence, and surrender. Little by little, he taught me about what each of these four words meant and how to live by them. As I searched my Bible, God ministered to me, giving me examples and verses to cling to. They were His promises for me, and ultimately what brought me to the point where I could be an overcomer. Each section contains thirteen verses from the Bible. I clung to these promises. My intent for you is to spend one week on each verse and reflection that goes with it. When I wrote this book I designed it with the following plan in mind.

Day One

Read the Bible verse several times and become comfortable with it. Then read the segment about my own journey of restoration and healing. But I want you to remember something. This book is not about me, but rather what God did for me as he gently and faithfully restored me. For years I wanted to write a book, but felt that if I wrote about myself, it would be self-centered. However, I found when

I relate my personal journey it has been a source of encouragement, hope, restoration and healing for others. We all share similar hurts and struggles at one time or another. At times you will be able to relate to some aspect of my story, or perhaps someone you know or love will have lived with that struggle. As I pray my way through this writing, it is my desire you will be encouraged and find hope.

Day Two

Read the Bible verse again. On this day I would like you to become comfortable the verse, when it was written and who it was written for. If you wish to dig deeper, look into the history behind the verse and gather any other information to help you understand what the biblical writer was saying. You may want to have a study Bible available to help you with this. Another helpful tip would be to look up verses referencing the theme verse of each reflection. When I do this, I am amazed how often there are Old Testament and New Testament passages relating to one another. This discovery affirmed to me that the Bible is real and truthful. Finally, write out the passage and place it where you will see it often.

Day Three

If you didn't write out the verse yesterday; do so today. Spend time memorizing it. Don't be concerned if the passage is a little longer and more difficult. Some of the verses may seem a little ridiculous to be memorizing. You may wonder what the verse has to do with anything! Trust the power of the Holy Spirit to speak to you through this verse. Also today, write the verse in your own words. How would it read if God himself were speaking it to you? You may want to keep a notebook handy and write in it as you study and memorize. In biblical times, the Jewish children had the Torah (the first 5 books of the Bible) entirely memorized by the age of 12. This was the only feasible way to make sure the Bible would not die, but continue for many generations to come since writing was not a part of their culture. What if you could memorize enough of God's Word to pass onto someone who could be encouraged and possibly be restored?

Day Four

Answer the questions accompanying each reflection. If you struggle with a certain question, make a note by it, pray about it and come back to it at a later time. We heal in different ways and at different times. If you get stuck there will be another opportunity for you to reflect on how to answer the question. Ask the Holy Spirit to guide you and in his way and time the answer will be there. The most important thing about these questions it to be totally honest with yourself. I would also encourage you to seek out a Christian life coach, pastor or other trusted person if you think you need the support, mentorship and encouragement of someone. There is no hard and fast timeline for how to work through these questions. Work through them at a pace allowing the Holy Spirit to do his deep and healing restorative work in you. If you are reading this book in a small group setting, confidentiality and trust is essential in the process of restoration.

Day 5

Read the final page, the words of hope and encouragement, as though your loving God is sitting next to you. Allow His presence to be felt and listen for Him to speak to your heart. Talk to Him about what you learned and discovered in this reflection. Say the Bible verse from memory to yourself. Finally, write down any other thoughts that come to mind and ask God to continue revealing his personal message of restoration for you. Quite often, God makes my ears perk up as I see or hear a particular Bible verse or passage more than once in a short amount of time. If you are new to reading the Bible, seek wise, godly counsel to help you understand what you are reading. Do not let a lack of biblical knowledge stop you in your journey of restoration.

I found the work of restoration to be hard work. As a physical therapy clinician, restoring patients to their highest level of independence possible is physically hard work. I restored furniture and renovated houses and this type of rehabilitation and renovation is not only tough, but messy too. It is pure toil as I work in my gardens; weeding, transplanting, pruning and shaping. And as I went through the hard work of emotional and spiritual restoration after painful life experiences, I found that too was difficult. Yet, eventually I found freedom. However, of all the restoration in my life, spiritual restoration has been the most difficult. But we have a God who is patient, compassionate and his specialty is being in the business of restoration. John vividly describes it in chapter five, verses one and two: *I am the true vine and my Father is the gardener. He cuts off every branch in me that bears no fruit, while every branch that does bear fruit he prunes so that it will be even more fruitful.* As God pruned and shaped, pursued and comforted me, slowly but surely, I discovered what it is really like to bloom!

It is a known fact we are spiritual, physical and emotional beings. Too often we try to heal and be restored in one or two of these areas, leaving a part of us un-restored in another. When I restore a piece of furniture it doesn't usually work to just put a new coat of varnish on the top if the legs are wobbly. Or when I work with a physical therapy patient, they will not really be restored if I do leg strengthening exercises with them, but don't teach them to walk again. Or when I coach a client, steps in the right direction won't happen if the work of answering questions isn't done. I encourage you to look at yourself in an honest way. Look for threads in your life where you are in need of spiritual restoration and how this can help emotionally and physically too. You will be given opportunities to do this as you reflect in this book. Above all, it is my prayer you will be able to take steps in the direction where God is leading you, that you will find hope and encouragement and that you will live as a restored creation of God, not just here on earth, but for all eternity.

SIMPLICITY

Simplicity

If you ever read a history book it doesn't take long to realize people have always viewed their lives as complicated. I am fascinated by this fact because so often we commiserate about how complicated life is today. I came to the conclusion about two things. When life is complicated and there is a desire for a simpler life, it becomes a matter of putting things into perspective. Secondly, there are things we can do to make life less complicated and there are even life coaches who specialize in lifestyle simplification. This section has thirteen reflections on simplicity and is meant for you to gain perspective and find spiritual value to help you physically and emotionally. Hopefully you will find ways to cope when life sneaks up from behind and tries to get complicated again. So I encourage you to think about simplicity, pray about what God will do for you, and through you during this time. Wait for our almighty and sovereign God to unravel the tangled web which makes life complicated.

Identity

I am the rose of Sharon, a lily of the valleys.
Song of Songs 2:1

There I sat, on the edge of my bed. My life was reeling out of control. I felt as though I was having a nightmare—a bad one. Only this was real. Just a year earlier, I had prayed that God would bring me to a place with him where I could know him more deeply and more intimately. I had been involved in many Bible studies over the years, and had a solid biblical foundation resulting from twelve years of parochial school. But I knew there was more. So I prayed that prayer. The next year my marriage disintegrated and I was bruised from betrayal and abandonment.

My two sons were struggling with what was happening and at the same time were finishing high school. Soon they would be getting ready to spread their wings and go off to college. Even our dog suddenly died. It is the stuff that sad songs are made of. I was too exhausted emotionally, spiritually and physically to pray or pick up my Bible. Nothing could console me and I had no purpose or reason to go on, nor did I know who I was anymore. Up to now my whole life had been wrapped up in my family and the roles that had gone along with it. Little by little, every one of them was gone, even the dog. Life had gotten chaotic and complicated.

As I got up from my bed that morning and made my way through the house, my eye caught a glimpse of the quilt hanging on the wall in the hallway. My mother had been a quilter and part of how she left a legacy was by making quilts. These quilts weren't hodge podge works, but designed specifically for the recipient and on the back side of each one she had stitched a message. The quilt she made for me is called the rose of Sharon. The design is intricately stitched with flowers resembling the rose of Sharon and then another layer of lilies of the valley is stitched around that. There is a large white circle surrounding the flowers, representing God's eternal, pure and perfect love. As I stood looking at this quilt, I longed for my mother who had died many years earlier. How I needed her right now! But I had her legacy to hold onto.

More importantly, God was showing his great love for me. He was sending me a message through that quilt. My first lesson about simplicity was to find out who I was. Through the help of a prayer ministry I began to be set free and for the first time in my life discovered my identity was not wrapped up in being Mrs. Kane, or Tim and Tony's mom, or somebody's physical therapist or any of the other hats I wore. It came down to the fact that I am the rose of Sharon. God was pursuing me. He was telling me that I am His beloved. No matter what happens on this earth, I am His!

The roles I played during my marriage and the time we were raising a family were temporary. I would have them for a season, but eventually these hats would change. My identity as a child of God and a daughter of the eternal king would never change.

Being the gardener I am, I wanted to know what the rose of Sharon was. It is believed that during the time before Christ, Sharon was a fertile coastal plain located south of Mount Carmel and lined the southeastern tip of the Mediterranean Sea. Some theologians believe the rose was a lily and others believe it was perhaps similar to a lotus or anemone. The anemones I grow in my garden are quite simple, yet beautiful. They have five well defined petals which spread out from a delicate and intricate yellow center, truly one of God's masterpieces. So as God called me to him and I would learn my first lesson about simplicity, it came down to this: I am the rose of Sharon, a lily of the valley. My roles in life would come and go, but my identity as a child of my heavenly father would never change. Little did I know the valley would continue for some time to come, nor did I know how much more God had to teach me about simplicity. But through the quilt on the wall He was showing me who I am. God was simplifying my identity, the first step in getting to know him intimately.

Who do you say you are?

Are you describing yourself by your roles or who you really are?

In the past when you wished you were someone else, what were you really saying?

What is one thing you can do to begin to understand who you really are in God's eyes?

Jayne Kane

A Call from God

Arise, my love, come away with me. Winter is gone and the rain from tears is done. I am bringing you flowers, the birds are singing with joy and you can hear the turtle doves cooing. The trees are budding and the vines are blooming with fragrance. A new season has come. Spring is here. Arise, my beloved and come away with me. (My paraphrase from Song of Songs 2:10-13)

You have many roles as you go about your everyday affairs. Do not confuse them with who you really are to me. I want you to know that you are my first love and you are all mine, if you will allow it to be. The world tells you that you need to wrap yourself up in roles making life complex and even chaotic. I want you to understand and put it in your heart that you are my lily. You are special to me; all I ask is that you make me the Lord of your life. It will simplify your identity and all the roles you hold will become more manageable when first and foremost you understand who we can be to each other. I will not stop pursuing you until you understand that you are my rose of Sharon. You are more beautiful than any flower that will fade after awhile. Your identity as my rose will be for eternity. I invite you to experience what living within the identity of being that beautiful, yet simple rose has to offer. So open your heart to me. Live a life of simplicity with the assurance you are all mine. Be with me and bloom as the rose of Sharon did.

4

Significance

Like a lily among the thorns is my darling
among the maidens.
Song of Songs 2:2

One of the most painful experiences a person can go through is being rejected. As I faced the struggled of a divorce I didn't want, I thought about other times in life when I had been rejected. I remembered the heartache of abandonment and rejection and what it felt like when the kids teased me in grade school, or when they wouldn't want to pick me for the team because I was too small. I felt unworthy, puny and insignificant. As my marriage disintegrated, the tapes from my past played in my head. I would go to sleep feeling unworthy and unlovable. In the morning the tape would start running again. It would go something like this: "I am not good enough. I am not worthy or lovable. No one will ever love me again." I convinced myself I would never be loved or accepted by anyone again and even the people who were still in my life would eventually *dump* me too. Feeling insignificant is the one struggle I battled all my life. If understood I was God's daughter then what was this thing of feeling insignificant? I was basing my emotions on the behavior of other people, not on the truth God was telling me through godly people and His word. But as I navigated through this valley of darkness, God ministered to me through the work of the Holy Spirit. He would say to me:

"You are the salt and light of the earth" Matt5:13, 14.

"You are my coworker" 2Cor. 6:1.

"I have chosen you, Jayne, to bear fruit" John 15:16.

My personal favorite and where significance began to come to life for me was when God told me I am a lily among thorns. I am significant even when there are thorns of rejection, abuse, abandonment, betrayal, hurts that cut to the soul and tears that flow, sometimes for no reason.

God was calling me his darling and saw me so significant (and beautiful) that I would stand out in his eyes!

I have some type of lily growing in nearly every one of my flower beds. Lilies are significant throughout the Bible and even thousands of years later are still one of the most beloved and recognized flowers of the garden. What makes lilies significant compared to roses are that they don't have thorns. Lilies are beautiful and have been blessed to not have thorns of rejection, abandonment, abuse or pain clinging to them. They wear the adornment of beauty and simplicity.

So little by little, through God's compassion and tender mercy, He would continue to show me I am His lily. I am His darling among the maidens. I count when it comes to God! I am so significant that God would compare me to the lilies He created; perfect, gorgeous colors, and unlike the roses, without thorns. Little by little, I would shed the negative image that had overtaken my mind that I don't matter. God would show up and bring healing and restoration to my life. He would prove to me that I am significant and worthy of His love for me. He would show me time and time again, I do count. He would demonstrate to me that I am His beautiful lily and one day again, I would bloom!

What thorns continue to hurt you and keep you from seeing your significance to God?

If you could be a flower or a workmanship of God (which you are, by the way) in nature, what would you be?

Everyone longs for significance. What in your life, realistically, makes you significant, and not just *feel* significant?

Even if you never did a thing of significance by earthly standards, what would make you significant in God's eyes?

My Pursuit

　　My lily, you are significant in my sight. You stand higher than the thorny plants of nettle or even the earthly roses of beauty. Rise higher than the thorns of abandonment, rejection, abuse and hopelessness. You are my mine and I have given you the most recognized and distinguished characteristics of all the flowers. I know how the thorns hurt you, the thorns that pierce and make your heart bleed. I wore a crown of thorns on my head at one time for you (Matthew 27:29). I too, faced rejection, abandonment and even death. I know how much those thorns hurt and make the heart bleed. The crown I wore was to remove the thorns of hurt you experience on this earth. But one day the earthly thorns will be replaced with a crown of beauty in heaven. So when your heart and flesh cry out for significance (Psalm 84:2) remember how I allowed thorns to be pierced into my flesh and to then be raised with the lilies in the most significant event of all time. You are worth it and you are significant to me. So for this time on earth I want you to stand tall and beautiful. Unlike the rose who has many thorns, you do not have thorns. You are as beautiful and as simple and as significant as the lily. Believe me when I tell you that you are significant. When the thorns of life make you feel insignificant, they are temporary. A crown waits for you in eternity; a crown of beauty making you significant forever!

Purpose

Consider how the lilies grow. They do not labor or spin.
Yet I tell you, not even Solomon in all his splendor was
dressed like one of these.
Luke 12:27

This is one of my favorite Bible passages; describing a vision of nature as God created it. This passage is from Jesus' famous Sermon on the Mount as he was teaching not only his disciples, but was also speaking to a multitude of people. When you read the verses before and after this verse, you will see that Jesus was laying out the blueprint for godly living. I love the heading in my NIV Bible at the beginning of chapter 12: *Warnings and Encouragement*. This is a wonderful balance of advice. As I listen to and encourage people in my coaching, there are three parts of our being people tend to struggle with. Those aspects are identity, significance and purpose. Take this time and reflect on what purpose is. Without a clear knowledge of purpose, a person tends to struggle with the reason for being or "What on earth am I here for?"

As Jesus was teaching on the hillside, I can just imagine the people sitting in the grass, lilies naturally rising up and growing with other vegetation in the landscape. Jesus used the lilies as an example to make his point. They were there for a purpose. They were growing to bring splendor and beauty to creation, even more beautiful than how Solomon, the richest man that had lived up to this time, had dressed. Then Jesus made a point about how these lilies lived. They did not labor or spin.

I love growing lilies in my garden. They are easy to grow; bringing beauty to the garden the first year they are planted. They are able to withstand the wind and drought the more fragile flowers can't tolerate. Lilies stand tall and carefree and best of all, they come in every color imaginable. They truly are the jewels of the garden. When I walk through the garden and take a moment to really look at them I am amazed at how complex and delicate these lilies are close up. Yet they are strong, simple and beautiful to the people who are driving or walking by.

Knowing our purpose in life, just as the lily knows its purpose, brings simplicity and focus to why we are here for this time on earth. Lilies grow for the purpose of bringing beauty to creation. They not only live out their purpose well, but they glorify and magnify God as they bloom. They live out his vision for creation as He designed it. Jesus told the people the lilies are even more beautiful than King Solomon. Solomon was the son of King David and was world renowned for his wisdom and insight. One of his purposes as king was to build a temple for worship in Jerusalem. At the height of his reign Solomon was wealthy, influential and still a man of integrity (1 Kings 4-9). As Jesus was comparing Solomon to the lilies he was saying their purpose was more significant and important than King Solomon was in all his glory as a king!

After my boys left for college, my husband was gone and I was burned out on work and career, I seriously questioned my existence and purpose. I had experienced another similar time in my life thirteen years earlier as I broke a cycle of abuse. Life did not seem worth living and purpose was the furthest thing from my mind. Even after God's amazing, divine intervention in my life when I experienced emotional and spiritual healing, I became deceived again as I went through more life losses. I lost a job, my life coaching was not developing and my family continued to experience pain (and I will even call it dysfunction) resulting from unresolved hurt. Life was complicated, chaotic and out of control. Purpose was nonexistent and was replaced by the need for survival. I was being anything but one of God's lilies during this time. Depression and even suicidal thoughts needed to be replaced with truth. And just as God brings the sunshine and the rain to the lily, so He brought His grace and love to me. He provided new insight for me in my work, gave me a new direction and passion for coaching and provided ways for me to express my desire to see His creation restored.

The lilies are a perfect part of God's creation and I am convinced we will see fields of them in heaven; every color imaginable. As I come back to living as the lily does, the simple truth is just as God created the lily for a purpose, God created you and me for a very specific one too. He has a plan and uses our past, our experiences and our gifts and abilities to accomplish His will for our lives. We need to begin by simply waving in the wind. Simplifying life and allowing God to be the Master Gardener is the first step in discovering purpose. Be encouraged by this. Tell yourself this as often as necessary and if you are questioning your purpose, begin the process of discovering what it is God has planned for you during this time on earth.

Do you know why God created you and put you here on earth?

What is your purpose? This is a loaded question. As you think about it, what are you telling yourself?

Are you spinning and laboring?

Or are you standing tall and colorful, waving in the breeze, more beautiful than Solomon in his glory?

If you are spinning and laboring, what is the first step you need to take to discover how God wants you to bloom?

The Master Gardener:

    Stop spinning and laboring, My Lily. Look around you. Stop and breathe and see my creation. Stop, if only for a minute and look at the beauty and simplicity life can bring. The lily understands its purpose and glorifies me through its beauty and existence and I desire that you would glorify me too. Walk with me through the lilies of the field and begin to discover that for everything I created there is a reason for my doing it. The lily comes in many colors, more beautiful than the gems that adorned King Solomon's clothes. I want you to understand you are more beautiful than all those jewels and more unique than even the most beautiful lilies that ever bloomed. I have in store for you a beautiful purpose, free of spinning and labor. Rest. Wave in the wind. As the sun and the spring showers make the lilies grow, so will my grace and mercy make you grow. Yes, even the rain of life can bring purpose and a reason for being to you. Search me and discover all the glory you can bring to me by living your purpose; your reason for being here today; for being planted for this season. I have blessed you with gifts, just as I did with Solomon and as I do even today. As my people the Israelites rebelled the prophet Jeremiah warned them that I will accomplish the purposes of my heart. Let this be a word of warning and encouragement to you also (Jeremiah 23:20). Stop laboring and spinning. This is a form of rebellion and will deter you from living out your purpose for me. You are my lily; my jewel. When you stop spinning and laboring I can bring meaning and purpose and simplicity to the chaos in your life. Allow me to be your gardener and through the help of my Spirit you will bloom!

Hindrances

Let us throw off everything that hinders and the sin that
so easily entangles and let us run with perseverance the
race marked out for us.
Hebrew 12:1

Living a life of simplicity can mean it is time to get rid of *stuff.* The stuff a person accumulates is unique to that individual. Sadly, there are people who have difficulty getting rid of their stuff; the materialistic things, possessions and the things that accumulate from living in our culture and on this earth. As a gardener, it is at times necessary to get rid of the invasive weeds that choke out the plants I am growing and hope to enjoy for years to come. Sometimes it happens that I have to remove plants and shrubs I still love, but have overtaken and outgrown the spot where they were planted. Recently, I discovered that a large spruce tree which protects the front yard from wind and the hot sun was being stunted by overgrown lilac and amur maple bushes. I didn't like the fact these bushes would have to be removed if the spruce tree was to thrive and grow. How I had enjoyed the fragrance of the blooming lilacs and the fall brilliance of the amur maples. Finally I made the decision that the bushes had to go.

So it can also be in life. Many times I struggled with tough life decisions of what may be hindering, entangling me and complicating my life. It was difficult to see the finish line in the race, because of stuff complicating my life. These hindrances kept me from running the race of perseverance. Pesky, bad habits allowed the enemy to have authority causing me to cling to things which gave me a false sense of security. Relationships entangled me and held me back and were hindrances in the race of perseverance.

Simplicity calls for making an honest assessment of what is entangling and hindering a person. When I am walking through my woods and see a weed winding around one of my woodland plants, I don't give a single thought to getting rid of the weed so the flower can once again thrive.

During a season when my heavenly father was disciplining me, a real desert time for me, I had to seriously assess some of the aspects of my character that was hindering and entangling me. I couldn't see the path in front of me because I was so hindered. I was being choked as a Christian who could run the race of perseverance and see the finish line. Anger and hurt from being abandoned in my marriage was a huge hindrance. I became entangled in the mistrust and disbelief God would protect and provide for me. The divorce was made even more complicated by gossip and rumors. This hindered me as I struggled with paranoia and fear. The most entangling sin hindering me though was anxiety. The root of most sin is fear and anxiety and sometimes it can be so deeply rooted a person is barely aware of it. This was the case with me. Even after God did his deep healing work of restoration, anxiety is still the one thing that will hinder me. It can consume me, so persevering is overwhelming and difficult to do. It can keep me from loving and living in the simplicity of God's love. It then prevents me from experiencing all he has in store for me in this race of life. When I confess and repent, I can allow the simplicity of God's love and the promises he gives to free me. All of the issues of daily life on this earth don't seem as complicated, especially when I know what is at the finish line: the promise of eternity with Jesus.

We removed the old lilac and amur maple bushes recently. The spruce tree is no longer hindered and can grow freely. The landscaping is once again free to grow, even though at one time the lilacs and maples brought beauty to that spot. This afternoon a rainbow cast its hues across the top of the spruce tree in this restored area. It was a reminder to me that God will always be with me, offering simplicity in life, that only *He* can. It is the simple promise that God will always be faithful and I need to throw away anything that hinders me from believing that promise. What a wonderful blessing this is as we run the race of perseverance without hindrances!

What entangles you and needs to be thrown away?

Is it a character flaw the healing blood of Jesus needs to take care of?

Is it a relationship that is keeping you from running the race God intended for you? Perhaps this relationship was at one time okay, but just as the lilacs and maples were once good, they eventually crowded the spruce from growing the way it was supposed to.

What is it that keeps you entangled in sin? Is it pride, fear or a false sense of security?

Is it complicating your life and hindering simplicity in your life?

Words in the Rainbow

My Dear One, the rainbow I send is to encourage you in your race of perseverance. Throw away all that is hindering you in that race. Remove the noxious weeds and vines that are complicating your life, your relationships and your love for me. I gave Noah the rainbow as a promise as he lived in simple obedience and perseverance, so I give you that same promise of my faithfulness to you (Genesis 9:12). Just as Noah had to leave behind all that was hindering him, so you must do the same. Living a life of simplicity, free of hindrances allows you to see the finish line. Not only that, it allows you to run the race with simplicity. As you gaze at the rainbow, enjoy the beauty and simplicity of it. Know that through all the colors of your life of living in simple obedience and perseverance I will be faithful and see you to the finish line. As your righteous God who searches and knows the character and motives of your heart (Psalm 7:9) and what may be hindering you, look to my promises in the Word. In search of the simple truths that will help you to run unhindered, you will find security and the ability to persevere when life becomes burdened, chaotic and entangled. Run the race of perseverance freely and unhindered. Follow the path I have set out for you. And one day, my righteous one, you will see the finish line of heaven. I will be waiting for you as you cross the finish line.

Staying Close

"Never will I leave you. Never will I forsake you."
Hebrew 13:5

This simple promise from God is a clear example of His love and faithfulness. I love that! It says God will *never* abandon or reject me. It is clear and simple and yet, so hard for me to believe at times. Shortly after my mom died, my first marriage ended in divorce. Six months after my divorce, my dad suddenly died, all happening in less than a year and a half. I wondered where God was. Ten years later I was diagnosed with an inoperable brain tumor. The following year my second husband left me and someone close to me was struggling with addiction. My faith was shaken again and I *really* wondered where God was. Along with this, there were all the other typical life events that everyone goes through. As is so often the case, these events tend to become magnified when life is already overwhelming. I came to a point where I could not combat the lies of abandonment and rejection. God knew this and He was about to demonstrate His love and faithfulness to me.

The truth is, God was and is always with you and me. I knew that, but knowing and believing it in my heart were two different things. The truth I knew and the lies the enemy told were two different things. I had this deep internal struggle within myself. Looking into this a little more revealed some things. The enemy knew I was weak and would attack me physically and emotionally. During those difficult times, I felt abandoned and rejected by God because I experienced loss, financial instability, insecurity and emotional lows in a number of areas. I became weakened spiritually, emotionally and physically. This led me to question where God was in all of this.

Have you ever been there? Perhaps it was at a time when there was no money, or during an illness or a struggle with chronic pain. Maybe it came when the one you love was no longer there. Perhaps you too, asked God if he left when someone betrayed you or was unfaithful to you or died. As humans, we tend to think of God our father in earthly terms. We connect our earthly fathers, parents and other mentors from the past to God. The truth is no matter what happened in the past or who hurt us, our heavenly father will never abandon or reject us. He is not an earthly type of father, but is divine in nature. God is perfect in every way.

Recently as I was reading through some of my writing when I lost a job, I came across an example of God's faithfulness to me. I had been at this job for nine years and most days I loved the work. This job loss was sudden and immediate. Of course the lies of rejection and abandonment attacked me again. The truth was our entire department had been eliminated. Another truth was this: God was allowing the loss to protect me from a situation that was going to become difficult. He was taking special care of me. Because He is an all knowing God, He knew what was best for me.

Initially, when I lost my job, I wasn't going to receive severance pay or any compensation. I had no idea how I was going to survive. At one of my lowest points, I woke up one morning and could barely face the day. As I poured out my heart to God and asked him where He was, He replied to me "Let me show my great love for you." How would He do that?

Less than an hour after my time with the Lord on this morning, the phone rang. The director of human resources from my former employer was calling to inform me that I would be receiving nine weeks of severance pay! *This* was how God was showing His great love and faithfulness to me. He was actively intervening as only God could and continued as my protector and provider. It was a simple demonstration of His love and faithfulness to me.

Where and when have you seen God's faithfulness to you? Did you think it was a stroke of luck or divine intervention? I don't seem to learn the simple lessons of God's faithfulness easily or quickly and this was definitely not the first time God had showed up in a big and timely way. There are so many examples over the course of my life where God demonstrated what I call my Hebrews promise. Here is another example.

Some years earlier, I had been in another difficult circumstance. I was totally alone financially, emotionally, physically and I thought spiritually. At the time I didn't know it, but God was hard at work in my life. I was faced with a second divorce, a mortgage and as sole provider for my two sons. It was all too big for me. On a particular July day I realized I was not going to be able to pay the mortgage for the month. I shared this hard truth with my teenage boys, explaining that somehow God would take care of us (but not really believing it my heart). I was totally exhausted and at a point where I didn't care anymore. But God was about to show up in a big way.

My pastor called to ask me if I could stop by the church to pick up an envelope left for me with my name on it. I had no idea what to expect. When I opened the envelope I found one thousand dollars in it! There was enough money to pay the mortgage for the month. Along with the money, was a note simply stating this was a gift from God. To this day I do not know where the money came from. God continued to be faithful and today I am still living in my house.

If you look closely at the entire verse in Hebrews 13:5 it says *"Keep your lives free from the love of money and be content with what you have."* Much of my struggle with feeling abandoned by God has been during financial struggles. But the truth is, even if I would lose all my material possessions, God would still provide for me and will never abandon or reject me. God will always be faithful to me. When I think about my weakness in not always believing God will never leave me, I think about Jesus hanging on the cross. Here was God's son, dying, basically alone and in the most awful way and under the most difficult circumstances. Jesus called out to God his father in heaven *"My God, my God, why have you forsaken me?"* Even Jesus, the holy and perfect son of God, felt abandoned and rejected at that point. God knows in my earthly and human state I will ask *"Why have you forsaken me?"* at times too. But when you see how God's magnificent plan unfolded, the temporary separation of abandonment and rejection Jesus experienced was for our eternal benefit.

God's simple promise says *"I will never leave you. I will never forsake you"*. We can come to the complete understanding the abandonment and rejection we experience here on earth is temporary and He will never leave or reject us as humans sometimes do. Even when everything is lost and gone here on earth, we have the promise that we will have eternity with God. What a beautiful, simple and eternal promise God is giving us!

What are the lies you tell yourself about rejection and abandonment?

What perspective do you have about God's faithfulness?

Do you see circumstances in your life as a *stroke of luck* or as God showing a *stroke of love* for you?

Can you cling to my Hebrews promise so the words are not only permeate your mind, but will also sink into your heart?

If you are having difficulty with the promise from God of His love and faithfulness for you, what is keeping you from believing it?

A Hebrews Promise

My child, I spoke to the Christians in the early New Testament and gave them the promise I would never leave them or abandon them; nor would I ever forsake them. I spoke this promise many times throughout Scripture. I am your heavenly Father, not of earthly means. I am unchanging and when I say never, I am saying it for all times sake. I was faithful to Noah, Abraham and David; to Ezekiel, Job and Jesus. In their humanness, they all questioned where I was. I see the anguish of your heart and the brokenness of your spirit just as I heard theirs. Even my people, the Israelites questioned my presence (Isaiah 65:14). The simple truth is I was always there for each of them, just as I am here for you today. Look around and see that even in the wilderness time of your life, I am providing water from the rock and manna for you, just as I did for the Israelites in their wilderness time (Exodus 16-17). Take this time and know even when you ask me why I have forsaken you, know that I continue to love you. My son, Jesus asked that question. But see how my grand plan worked out, not only for his good, but for my glory! This plan is meant for you. My seemingly temporary separation from Jesus was so you would not be separated from me into eternity. Believe this with all your heart. I will never leave you. I will never forsake you. I love you too much to do that to you.

A Dwelling Place

Even the sparrow has found a home and the swallow a nest for herself, where she may have her young—a place near your altar, Oh Lord Almighty, my King, and my God.
Psalm 84:3

Growing up on a farm meant that home was much more than just the house. Our farm was arranged so the house, barn and other buildings were within close walking distance of each other. A grove of trees my dad planted surrounded the farm buildings and yard and acted as a buffer from the snow and wind. Corn and hayfields covered the rolling hills beyond the grove. And of course there was the pasture. The birds that built their nests on the farm were a natural and important part of it. Some of my earliest memories were the house wrens and purple martins who made their nests in the houses my dad built. Then there were the pesky barn swallows that swooped down at us when we walked into the barn. They were noisy and invasive as their nests were built of mud and straw. Between the dried mud and bird droppings that fall from the nest it isn't desirable to have one near by. There was also the Baltimore oriole who had the hanging nest in the old elm tree by the house. This nest was constructed as a unique basket like structure, intricately woven together, and swinging freely from a limb that stretched far beyond the tree trunk. It was difficult to detect and as it swung precariously it looked as though it could fall any second.

As the Psalmist was writing this verse in chapter eighty four, he must have also been observing the common sparrows and swallows, making their nests near the temple Solomon built. Here were the most ordinary and common birds; sparrows and swallows. The writer doesn't say why these birds could be in the temple, but he couldn't be. For some unknown reason he was unable to be a part of the dwelling place of the Lord.

Having a *dwelling place* should be simple and easy. Everyone is entitled to a dwelling place, the place to *be* in, to *go to,* for protection and provision. Nests are the safe places for birds, and our homes and places of worship should also be safe places; physically, emotionally and spiritually. The psalmist in this verse is referring to the temple, the house of God in his time. Commentators have not been able to determine what was keeping the writer from having access to it. Have you ever been in a place where you do not have access to God's house? Perhaps you never had a *safe* place to go to worship God. Or the place of worship you visited or were a part of was so complicated with ritual, legalism, or ungodly attitudes and behaviors that the true meaning of worship was nearly impossible to express or experience. Just as some bird nests are messy and complicated and even a nuisance, a place of worship can also be messy. Churches are made up of humans, sinful in nature and because of this fact there are times when sinful human nature gets in the way of God's plan for the community of faith. However, God wants us to be a part of corporate worship where Christians can be in community with one another. Perhaps that is why the Old and New Testament writers spent so much time writing about the physical, spiritual and emotional aspects of the corporate faith community.

Worshipping in God's house is only a part of what God really wants. What God truly desires is to be in relationship with us. He wants us to *commune* with him, which is to be in a real and personal relationship with him. Worship is not about just going to church and going through the motions and it certainly shouldn't be a place where either overt or subtle spiritual abuse takes place. Having been without a church home at two separate times in my life, I learned some life lessons about what it really means to be in His *dwelling place.* Being without a church home forced me to examine what I wanted from being a part of a faith community. It allowed me to experience God's nearness, even when I didn't have a spiritual *nest;* a dwelling place to go to. It made me examine what I was doing in my own worship life. Ironically, as so often is the case, through divine intervention, I learned what the Old and New Testament core of worship was all about.

This revelation came when I was going to school to complete my bachelor's degree and one of the classes I took was on worship. I was struggling with a situation at church that had left me feeling battered, bruised, confused and hurt. There were no easy answers and I was able to relate to the psalmist who was questioning why the common (and messy) swallows and sparrows could be a part of the temple. Can you relate to this? Perhaps the church betrayed you or was not a spiritually healthy or safe place to be. Maybe you were separated from your faith community because of your stand on an issue or the decisions made did not agree with your biblical world view. Possibly you moved and you were left searching and yearning for a church such as the one you left.

Here is the simple truth about being in the dwelling place with God. It is not about the physical structure or the people who belong to it. It is all about God and your relationship with Him. Once I removed myself emotionally and physically from my faith community, God was able to do a deep work of restoration in me. As I learned about the holiness of the tabernacle when the Israelites were wandering in the wilderness, my own understanding of reverence for God and my attitude towards worship changed and deepened. As I struggled, I questioned if I would ever be a part of a faith community again. After being betrayed by two different churches with very different dynamics, I came to the understanding of the interdependence of private and corporate worship. I searched for a godly model of what a faith community representing how God ordained the organized church to be. He met me there and provided for me. I came to understand whenever I entered into private worship with an attitude of praise I was in the dwelling place with God. This private, holy place without the limits of time or interferences of the outside world was a safe place for me. Once I started attending a church again, I was able to say as the psalmist did: "*O Lord Almighty, my King and my God.*" Worship life for me had been restored to a simple place of safety. I had a dwelling place, a safe haven and nest where I could be with my king, privately and corporately.

A couple of years ago a barn swallow built a nest on my front porch. Usually it is one of the few nests I will knock down and destroy because it is messy and a nuisance. Once the babies hatch they are noisy and the droppings land on the front step. But for some reason I didn't have the heart to get rid of this one, partly because a single swallow eats thousands of insects and mosquitos and their feathers are tinted in beautiful, yet subtle tones of turquoise and purple. Each time I went in and out the front door the swallows swooped at me as they fed their young, just as they did at my dad when he went into a barn. Today the nest is still perched under the eave of my porch as a reminder that God cares for the swallows too. It is no longer used by the swallows because they build a new one every season. Sometimes as I listen to their chatter as they perch on the power line running along my property line I imagine they are in a dwelling place, singing their praises to God, even though their nest sight is no longer accessible or usable.

What does your worship experience with God look like in your life?

Do you worship corporately in a faith community or privately in the dwelling place of your heart? Both or neither?

Do you have burdens, hurts, barriers or other complicating matters keeping you from being able to be in the dwelling place with the Lord?

Is your worship experience like a swallow's nest, messy and complicated or more like the Baltimore oriole's dwelling place, free, yet hanging in the balance of total dependence on God?

Dwell With Me

    Enter into the dwelling place of simplicity with me, your God. Be in that safe place of my care and guidance and know that all I want is your worship and adoration. Yes, the organized church can be messy and complicated without the deep restoring work of the Holy Spirit. But because of my care for you, know that I am more concerned with the dwelling place in your heart. That is why I want Christ to dwell in your hearts through faith (Ephesians 3:17). Even the common sparrows and swallows have a dwelling place and I will not deny you that. But I am more concerned about the dwelling place of your heart than of the physical structure of sticks and stones King Solomon built. Come and be with me. Praise me without the nest. Worship me in spite of outward circumstances and know that I love your praises just as much as I love the singing of the birds in the early summer morning. Yes, it is true, I want believers to worship and be in community together. But the dwelling place of the church cannot be the nest I designed it to be until each believer has me in the dwelling place of their hearts. Search for me in that dwelling place and be encouraged. I will guide, protect, and love you just as the mother bird does with her young. Come to the dwelling place that is always accessible and you will be blessed!

Instructions

"Take nothing for the journey except a staff—no bread,
no bag, no money in your belts."
Mark 6:8

Have you ever gone some place where you could take only what was absolutely necessary? It is a difficult thing to do since we think we need so much, living in the complicated and overindulgent world we do. This verse in Mark chapter six is an interesting verse, a quote from Jesus himself as he was giving direction to his disciples for how they were to travel in their ministries. What would you take if you were told you could take only one thing on a trip?

There was a time and situation in my life when I was faced with taking a minimum amount of stuff with me on a journey. I was in an emotionally and physically abusive relationship. It had escalated to a dangerous level and professional counselors and law enforcement advised me to remove myself from the environment before it would escalate to a point of *no return.* I was scared, uncertain and not sure of what the future held. All I knew was I wanted to keep my two little boys with me and that God would be *my staff.* That experience was a life changing one. It made me realize what my priorities were and how trivial and unimportant most of what I have here on this earth really is. So then why is it so difficult to live with this perspective of simplicity in everyday life?

This longing for a life of simplicity was intensified every time I went on vacation to one of my favorite places in northern Minnesota. As I sat by the campfire, listening to the loons calling in the distance or on the quiet shores of the lake watching the sunset, life seemed simple and care free. I continually asked myself the question, "What can I do to live my life in simplicity? How can I capture these simple moments on my vacation and take it back to daily living?"

Jesus was called a simple man because he had no home, no possessions and took only what he needed for survival when he traveled. As I read Mark 6:8 I reflected on the staff. Was the staff more important than money? What is the significance of the staff? In the Bible, people traveled with a staff to guide them and hold them up as they walked over the hard, rocky, treacherous terrain. That region of the world is very rough and dry. Predators, such as snakes lurk between the rocks. Travelers could use a staff for stability as they climbed the rocks or they could use it to ward off snakes and other varmints that were a potential threat or harm to them. Once the traveler, or in this case the disciples, arrived in the city or town they were being sent to, they stayed with believers in Christ who would take care of them and supply the disciples with whatever they needed during their stay. The host family did not expect money for their hospitality. It was their way of supporting the advancement of the Gospel and was a true demonstration of how Jesus wanted his people to live. What a simple way to live!

In reflection of this concept, what parts of our lives need to be simplified? Of course, living in the culture we do, it is nearly impossible to live as the disciples did. But the concept of living a simpler life is not unattainable in our culture. Entire books have been written on this subject and some life coaches specialize in this area. There is one principle that truly captures what is at the heart of living a simpler life. It is found in the staff.

When I go for walks in the woods, I sometimes grab a stick to be a *helper*, especially if I am going into the deeper woods behind my property where the ravine drops down to the river. The staff acts as my guide and keeps me from falling. In reality, when I go on one of these walks, all I really need is a walking stick. I don't need money or even a bag. It helps if I put mosquito repellent on before I leave and of course, I wear my best and favorite pair of walking shoes. But the most important thing I need is the walking stick.

David says in Psalm 23, *"You are my rod and my staff."* The staff in this case is God and as a shepherd, David understood the value of the staff. It supported him as he led his sheep over the rocky hills and it also acted as an aid when one of the sheep strayed off the path and needed to be brought back to the rest of the flock. So, fast forward thousands of years after David, Jesus was telling the disciples to take only a staff with them as they journeyed from town to town.

In the day and time when I fled with my two little boys, I took only the essentials I needed to survive the next five days. I will admit I took whatever money I could scrape together, some clothes and food and a few toys for the boys. By far the most important item I took with me was my Bible. In retrospect, God and His Word was my staff. I was in a total state of dependence on Him to provide for my needs at that time, and all I knew was that I just needed to live in obedience and follow His lead. And in the end, the situation was resolved in a way far better than I ever imagined.

Living as I do today, I have so much! I am living the dream I had as a child, of having a home in the country with trees and gardens and flowers. But I will admit, I struggle with the materialism of our culture and of living in total dependence on God. I don't always rely on the *rod* and *staff* of God's Word and direction from Him with the help of the Holy Spirit to give me guidance and reproof. But when I do rely on Him, life is simpler and less complicated, even though the closets are still full of *stuff*. It brings me back to my times at the lake, listening to the loons when I leave all the stuff and become totally dependent on God to give me direction and insight for the journey ahead.

What is the *stuff* in your life you need to leave behind for the journey ahead?

Do you see the rod (reproof) and staff (guidance) from the Bible as a way to simplify your life?

If you had to leave your home for five days, not knowing what the future will hold for you, what would you take with you?

Do you desire a simpler life or have you resigned yourself to "this is just how it is"?

What step do you need to take to become more dependent on God and less dependent on materialistic things?

The Guide

As you journey through life, take me with you as your rod and staff. Become totally dependent on me and leave everything else behind. Learn to use my Word and the prompting of my Spirit to guide you, just as you would use a staff when you are walking. Hear my voice through Scripture and the Holy Spirit will bring clarity and purpose to the stuff in your life. I am with you, My Lamb. Whether you are fleeing the storms of life, living in the difficult days of perseverance or flying on a high cloud of joy and happiness, living a life of simplicity is essential. Yes, the falling rocks, the snakes and the unknown twisting turns in the path will lurk, but living in a state of total dependence on me will simplify the journey. Just as I instructed my disciples to take only a staff with them, so I am telling you the same. You will gain understanding, you will know my will for your life and your heart will be obedient. You will find that my directing you will bring delight to your life. So allow your heart to be directed and put away the desire for earthly gains and worthless stuff (Psalm 119:34-37). Reflect on what you really need for the journey and leave the rest behind. I am with you and will meet your needs. As your provider, I specialize in hospitality and I know ahead of time what you will need on the road. So pick up your staff and follow my lead. Enjoy the journey and keep it simple. I am with you!

Fruit

The fruit of the Spirit is love, joy, peace, patience,
kindness, goodness,
faithfulness, gentleness, and self control. Against such
things there is no law.
Galatians 5:22

Some years ago, I purchased a small house in the country and one of the first things I did was plant an orchard. My dad had just passed away and the farm I grew up on had been sold. I missed going home to the farm to pick the apples, pears, cherries and grapes Dad had grown over the years. When I planted the orchard I knew it would take some years for the trees to mature and bear fruit, so it was high on my list to plant them as soon as possible. I planned, planted, pruned and watered. I wrapped the trunks to protect the bark from being eaten and damaged by rabbits and deer. And I frequently checked the leaves for insects and other pests.

Today the trees in my orchard supply enough fruit for my family, neighbors, friends and co-workers. It gives me great joy to give apples and pie cherries away and I am teaching my nieces to make grape jelly. It saddens me when the deer and rabbits chew on the bark, or hail and insects damage the leaves and fruit, stunting the growth of the fruit and limiting the trees potential.

The fruit of the Spirit can be compared to the fruit trees in an orchard. The fruit needs to be tended and nurtured too. Regular attention has to be given to the trees in order for them to bear fruit although some fruits such as pears and cherries are relatively easy to care for. Others such as apples are more prone to insects and need additional attention. The same can be said for the fruits we want to bear in our lives.

Many good studies and teachings have been written on this Bible passage and it is a key life principle when it comes to living a life of simplicity. For me, fruit of the spirit is difficult to live by consistently. But God in His goodness, grace, mercy and love for me knows that. Here is an example of how well He knows me. Sometime back in one of my times with the Lord, He gave me four words. I quickly scribbled them on a piece of paper, not knowing exactly what those words would lead to. In the days, weeks and months following I came to know why God gave them to me. They are related to the fruits of the spirit and were critical for me in becoming the life coach he wanted me to be. Those four simple words are listen, compassion, gentleness and prayer. As they correlate to the fruits of the Spirit they could be interpreted as self control by listening, rather than talking (all the time), kindness by being compassionate, gentleness at all times so trust is not destroyed and faithfulness in prayer. Today that scribbled little piece of paper hangs above my desk and frequently I find the Holy Spirit prompting me to put into practice one or all of them at the same time.

As I look at the fruits of the Spirit in Galatians I can tell you which ones are easier for me to live by and which ones I need to prune, water and take extra time to tend to. Sometimes relationships and circumstances are complicated and need extra attention because the fruits of the Spirit are not being practiced. As human beings, we are shaped by life experiences as well as the genes we inherit and the way God created us. All this put together makes us the people we are. Just as a tree is shaped by the management of the orchard grower, we as people of God can be shaped through the power of the Holy Spirit.

There is one key to the passage as we look at the fruits of the Spirit. It is *only* with the help of the Holy Spirit that any of us can bear fruit. The fruit of the Spirit does not mean that it comes from our own doing or efforts. Nor is it pulled from somewhere within. It comes only from the Spirit of God. Admittedly, some days I do better with the fruits of the Spirit than on other days. But because I am totally human, I need the continuous special nurturing of the Holy Spirit to truly produce those fruits. This is especially true when I am physically or emotionally struggling.

When I am tending to my orchard, I check to see what each tree needs. Some trees may need a new bark protector or a dose of insecticide or perhaps a little extra water. Or the fruit that fell and is lying underneath the tree is rotting away and has to be picked up. And sometimes all the tree needs is something I can't give it—sunshine! The fruits of the Spirit are the same way. It is only with the sunshine of the Holy Spirit that healthy and godly fruit can be produced.

Since the day I received the four words of fruit from God, I adopted a practice of simplicity that helps me to live out the fruits of the Spirit. When I am in a difficult situation I quietly pray for the Holy Spirit to give me whatever fruit I need to me get through. Sometimes I just need to listen. At other times being gentle or compassionate can change things. But it is always with the help of the Holy Spirit, not my own doing.

An important part of growing an orchard is to maintain the growth around the trees. So I pick up the fallen fruit before it rots, mow the grass around it and prune away weeds that could eventually affect the growth and vitality of the trees. When it comes to bearing the fruit of the Spirit there are many comparisons. I learned that at times it is necessary to discern if a relationship, circumstance or other outward factors would not be healthy or godly for me. Sometimes simplicity means getting rid of the bad fruit that threatens my own fruit of the Spirit. At the time, it can seem like hard work and making the choices can be critical. But life is complicated, so why keep bad fruit around when there is so much good fruit to enjoy? It is important when it comes to bearing the fruit of the Spirit and it is a basic principle of living a life of simplicity.

Which of the four fruits of the Spirit would you pick that requires special nurturing in your life?

What is the bad fruit in your life? Are there certain relationships, situations or dynamics that are pesky, invasive and keep you from bearing good fruit?

What outward factors or situations threaten the orchard where your fruits of the Spirit have potential for growing and living in simplicity?

Do you view the Holy Spirit as the only orchard grower in helping you produce fruit of the Spirit or do you try to do it by yourself?

From the Orchard Grower

 Let my Spirit be upon you! Bask in the sunshine of my presence and soak it up. Grow in your love and knowledge of me so the fruit that is produced seems almost natural. The fruit that is produced seems simple in nature, love, joy, peace, patience, kindness, goodness, faithfulness, gentleness, self control. But I know it takes work, pruning, water, protection and fertile soil for the fruit to bear. As you bear fruit, I ask you to desire the things it takes to bear good fruit. Allow me as your grower to prune and water you as grow in my presence. As you bear good fruit through my Spirit you will see the fruits of your labor multiplied and many will be blessed. Just as a bushel of apples will feed and bless many, so will the good fruit you bear. Yes, the winds, the hail, pests and harsh winters will try to prevent you from bearing good fruit, but as your protector and through the sunshine and working of the Holy Spirit, my promise of good fruit will prevail. So be a blessing to others with your fruit of the Spirit. You in return will be a blessing to me and in return you will be blessed too. My kingdom is of righteousness, peace and joy in the Spirit, and when you serve me in this way you are pleasing me and approved by men (Romans 14:17).

A Little

Better the little that the righteous have than the wealth
of many wicked.
For the Lord loves the just and will not forsake his
faithful ones.
Psalm 37:16, 28

Psalm 37 is one of the Psalms that became a love letter from God for me. This Psalm has ministered to me, healed me and restored me through times when I could not make sense of what was happening; much less see a glimmer of hope for the future. I adopted Psalm 37 as my personal encouragement chapter and I will always remember the day I read this Psalm and knew God was speaking to *me.* It was during a famine time as it says in verse 19 and it was one of my low, lonely and hard times. We all have them at one time or another and many people in the Bible went through those hard times. One example is Job who was probably one of the most renowned biblical characters to have endured a famine time. The book named after him is devoted to his story. During the time of famine I was going through, there just didn't seem to be any justice in my life. Every time I turned around there seemed to be another crisis. Spiritually, emotionally, and physically I was in a famine. According to the principles of our culture and from outward appearances it appeared that I was blessed. But inwardly I was depleted.

It was March, a generally dreary month in Minnesota. Winter was dragging on. Work was drudgery and my job was unstable. My work hours had been cut and the rumors were swirling at work. To say the least, finances were difficult. I was lonely, getting only occasional phone calls from friends. Adding to all of this, a dear friend and prayer partner was sick. And to top it all off, circumstances at my church were forcing me to evaluate what was spiritually healthy for me as I clung to the hope that perhaps things would work themselves out and I wouldn't need to make a change. These trials were not unique to just me. And perhaps at this point you may be saying, "Yes, yes, amen!" I was lamenting the fact that life is not fair! For anyone who has been on this earth for any length of time this is not news. It is simple truth, life is not fair. If I came up with a list of adjectives to describe what was happening, it would go something like this: unfair, wrong, hard, evil, unjust, demoralizing, sinful, painful, bad, harmful, etc.

As I read Psalm 37 God gave me insight and hope and began to change my thinking. And as he transformed my thinking, restoration began to happen. Circumstances and events weren't changed, but my thinking and perception was being changed. So it went something like this. I am a victim, but I want to survive this. What I really want though, is to do more than just survive. I want to overcome this! The presence and grace of God was washing into my life and I realized that I had choices (and maybe my German stubbornness was kicking in a little too). I was not going to allow life to defeat me and I wanted to do more than just survive. I wanted to overcome! So I was faced with a multiple choice question.

a) be a victim
b) be a survivor
c) be an overcomer

We are all faced with this multiple choice question at some time in life. It is inevitable that life circumstances and situations will force us to answer the question "What do you want to be?" It is during those defining moments that our free will gives us the ability to choose the path we will take. I am the first to admit the choice is not always easy. And even at the moment I chose to be an overcomer, I found myself wanting to revert back to being a victim of life again. It seems easier and simpler to be a victim. Overcoming takes work, patience, perseverance, faith and a trust that God will make things right in His own way and time. Even up to this time of writing I find myself thinking there must be a simpler and easier way to get to the top of the mountain of overcoming. There must be a shortcut to being an overcomer and victor on the mountain top rather than continuing to be a victim of life.

When was the last time you had a mountain top experience, the kind that takes your breath away and leaves you with goose bumps on your arms? I remember my first trip to the Black Hills of South Dakota. I had been to other mountain ranges that are far more spectacular than the Black Hills, but there is one particular mountain unique to the Black Hills. My husband and I were driving along the Needle Nose Highway on a beautiful late spring day. We had the top of our convertible down and around each bend of the narrow road we had a picture postcard view of the mountains. At one point my husband slowed the car down and pulled over to the side of the narrow road. He pointed to an open area in the trees and said "Look over there." Between the foliage of the trees I saw Mount Rushmore, bigger than life and more majestic and beautiful than any picture I had ever seen of it. It was truly a mountaintop experience!

That glimpse of mountain majesty when I didn't expect it is what living life as an overcomer is like. Being an overcomer is a journey of twists and turns. The challenges don't change and life can be just as chaotic and unpredictable as ever. But through the eyes of an overcomer, each twisty turn of life is viewed as a picture postcard event. And every so often there will be a mountaintop experience. It brings life back into a state of simplicity and righteousness.

Back to the March day sitting in my living room as I made the decision I wanted to be an overcomer. Figuratively, I wanted to see glimpses of beauty and majesty again. I was sick and tired of the famine. Psalm 37 provided those glimpses from an overcomer's view point; *"Better the little that the righteous have than the wealth of many wicked (Verse 16). The days of the blameless are known to the Lord (Verse 18). In times of disaster they will not wither; in days of famine they will enjoy plenty (Verse 19). The Lord will make his steps firm (Verse 23) The Lord upholds him with his hand (Verse 24). For the Lord loves the just and will not forsake his faithful ones (Verse 28). There is a future for a man of peace (Verse 37)."*

This gives us a glimpse of the picture postcards from God's view of what life is like for His overcomers.

Even when there seems to be famine, and righteousness, goodness and peace are hard to come by, there are promises of hope to live by. When wrong seems to be winning and wickedness continues to prevail, there is encouragement. Psalm 37 is the map for moving beyond being a victim and even a survivor and ultimately to be at the mountaintop where you can shout "I am an overcomer!!!!!!" It puts life as we know it into perspective; God's perspective that is. I came up with a little formula that is the key to all of this.

Living right with God (having the perspective of an overcomer) even when there is little that is right = wealth.

Living in disobedience (continuing in a victim role, not how God wants us to live) = only seeming like wealth.

As I unraveled the truths of God's justice based on my time in Psalm 37, life became a whole lot simpler. It made it easier to move beyond being a victim or even just a survivor and it somehow set things right when there really wasn't anything going right at the time. The twists and turns of that time in my life could have been compared to the twists and turns of the Needle Nose Highway. What I needed to do was to look to Psalm 37 for mountaintop experience of being an overcomer, just as the mountain top experience of Mount Rushmore. The view from the mountaintop as an overcomer is majestic and it brings life into the focus of simplicity. The perspective of an overcomer is a mountaintop experience before reaching the mountaintop itself!

Take the test and be totally honest with yourself. Do you see yourself as

a) a victim
b) a survivor
c) an overcomer

When was the last time you had a mountaintop experience -
Physically (you can answer this even if you have never seen a mountain)

Emotionally

Spiritually

37

What in your life has not been or is currently not fair?

What in God's eyes would He want you to do to come into a state of *wealth,* not monetarily speaking of course?

How do you picture your life as an overcomer?

Which verses in Psalm 37 can you claim for yourself as an overcomer?

On Overcoming

My righteous one, I have overcome, through my son Jesus, so that you may be an overcomer. I know there are times when it seems as though the ungodly are blessed with wealth. But I want you to know that as you live a righteous life in me and with me, you won't have just a little, but that you will be blessed in ways you never thought of before. From my perspective you don't have just a little, but you have wealth that cannot be measured monetarily. I understand the parts that have been wrong. I know how you have been wronged. I am not blind to the evil, unjust and unfair. I know how wickedness seems to prevail and it seems as though the wrong seem to get by and even get richer. But this is just for awhile. I am a just God. And as you claim your victory as an overcomer, you will have a new perspective from the mountaintop. You will see that a victim who stays a victim will in the end have nothing. As an overcomer you will have vantage points and insights based on the Truths I have given you in Scripture. And with the help of my Spirit you will have mountaintop experiences as an overcomer that you never expected. I encourage you to seek that which is truly right and leave justice to me. My justice will prevail and even though this may be a time of famine, there is the promise of plenty in the future. Take heart and claim your victory as an overcomer, in my son Jesus, who overcame all that was (John 16:33) and is and will be. Rest in that fact and enjoy life as an overcomer from the mountaintop.

Being Forgotten

Are not five sparrows sold for two pennies? Yet none of them is forgotten by God. Indeed, the very hairs on your head are numbered. Don't be afraid; you are worth more than many sparrows.
Luke 12:-6-7

Growing up on a farm without playmates close by meant that I had to invent things to do and one of my favorite pastimes was looking for feathers. We usually had ducks, geese and chickens around the yard, so their feathers were easy to find. However, finding feathers from the song birds was a little more difficult. To find those feathers I had to tromp through the grove of trees and hunt through the tall grass. One summer a robin built her nest in the old elm tree just outside the front door. This mother robin was protective of her nest and would chatter and scold if I tried to sit on the old wooden swing that hung from the tree branch close to where she had built her nest.

And then there were the gold finches. I would beg my dad to catch one of these so I could put it in a cage and keep it as a pet. A great aunt of mine had parakeets and I thought the gold finches resembled them. But my dad explained that the gold finches were meant to be left outside to swing from the thistles and that they were much happier there than if I kept them a cage. I have to smile a little as I look up from my writing to watch the gold finches eating at my thistle feeder. Watching these little yellow birds is a reminder of the simplicity of God's creation as they freely swing from the feeder without a care in the world.

Just beyond the thistle feeder in my front yard I can see the bluebirds on the lawn, picking insects to take to their little ones. It is no wonder they are nicknamed bluebirds of happiness as they flit about taking care of their young, doing what God created them to do. Interestingly, bluebirds were nearly extinct when I was growing up. My dad built bluebird houses and put them up, but we never had any that occupied those houses. Were they forgotten by God? How could something so good be forgotten? Perhaps if the bluebirds could have talked during those days of near extinction, these are questions they would have asked.

Through the hard times in my life I have asked the question too. Have you forgotten me, God? There were nights when I would lie in bed crying after an episode of violence, crying as much from the emotional wounds as the physical ones. I would sob in my pillow, asking God "Where are you?" And there were times after the divorce when there was no money in the checking account and the bills were not paid and I would ask God "Have you left me?" During those times I was convinced God left me. I was bringing God down to a human level and subconsciously was putting Him in the same category as the people who had let me down.

But God, in His infinite mercy and grace and love for me always came through. For example, after my mom died God brought godly women into my life who reminded me of her. Of course, no one could replace her, but these godly women would provide for me some little part of who she had been to me. There were friends who were good listeners and others who had godly wisdom. There were others who were well-versed in Scripture and could encourage me with Bible verses. And there were women who had quilted with my mom and could tell me stories of their times together and about the legacy she left. Even today, nearly twenty years after she died I have people in my life who mentor and are a sort of mother to me.

One small example of this came seemingly out of the *blue*. I went to see a physical therapy patient in her home. As she welcomed me in her home, I noticed the many quilts she displayed. I told my patient about my mother's love of quilting and through a short conversation, we discovered she and my mom had been quilting *sisters*. My patient knew of me and in our mutual discovery, said I resembled my mom. We shared our grief of our loss and found comfort in the fact that God does not forget about us and knew our meeting had been orchestrated through divine intervention. This meeting came at a time when I was struggling with the finalization of my divorce and was wishing for comfort from my mom and questioning God about where He was.

As an encourager, I enjoy telling people this story. Struggling with being alone in the chaos of a fallen world, it is sometimes be difficult to see God at work and it is easy to think that God doesn't remember or care about us. Jesus, in his infinite wisdom, knew this as He spoke to crowds of people. Even back then, people needed to hear the simple truths of God. When you read Luke 12, Jesus was telling the people they were worth more than the sparrows which were sold cheaply for food. The sparrows, feathers and all were created by God and for that matter so were the gold finches and the blue birds.

The bluebirds are making a comeback and are no longer an endangered species. There are two families of them occupying the houses I have on my lawn. Their feathers are fascinating because the color is actually a bluish gray and when you hold a feather in the sunlight it takes on the hue of a brighter blue. I still enjoy occasionally walking around my yard collecting feathers. It is a reminder to me that God cares for me as much as he does for the birds he created. As Jesus talked to the crowds about the simple truth that God knows how many hairs we have on our heads and that He cares for us so much more than the sparrows, this simple truth is still true for us today. My feather collection today consists of sparrow, blue jay, robin, pileated woodpecker, cardinal, wild turkey, downy woodpecker, bluebird and gold finch feathers. God has not forgotten about his birds or his people and has not forgotten about you or me.

In what life circumstances have you found yourself asking God, "Where are you?"

What have you been telling yourself when you ask this question?

Can you see God at work in your life, even when chaos and problems are overwhelming?

As you read and memorize the Luke 12:6-7 verses, do you believe the simple truth that you are not forgotten by God?

I Know Your Hairs

My precious one, I know and care for you. I created the birds as well as all of the beauty of creation surrounding you. The feathers of the birds are unique and intricately placed. Even the feathers of the common sparrow are. I continue to love all of creation and provide for it. As the bluebird once again thrives and contributes to the glory of my creation, so does my desire for you. You may question your survival—emotionally, spiritually and physically. You may be feeling close to being extinct. But remember this truth: you are not forgotten and nothing can separate you from my love (See Romans 8:35). Speak this truth of simplicity to yourself until it becomes a part of your being. And then look around to see me at work. I know exactly how many hairs you have on your head as well as everything else about you. I even know your needs before you are aware of them (Matthew. 6:8). And I know your longings even better than you do. It may be unsettling to you that I even know about the darkness in your life. My mercy and grace is available to take care of the darkness. But rest assured I have not forgotten about you. There is an abundance of sparrows and I haven't forgotten about a single one. And even when there seems there is little to rejoice in, I continue to provide for all of my creation. Do not be afraid. Neither the sparrows nor the bluebirds are.

Reconciliation

All this is from God who reconciled us to himself through Christ and gave us the ministry of reconciliation: that God was reconciling the world to himself in Christ, not counting men's sin against them. And he has committed to us the message of reconciliation. We therefore are Christ's ambassadors.
2 Corinthians 5:18-20

Being from Minnesota, I have done a fair amount of fishing in my life time. I have many memories of sitting in my Grandpa's boat with him, spending hours fishing for sunfish, crappies and bass. But as much as I remember fishing, I also remember the stories he told me of growing up during the Great Depression, serving in World War II, surviving floods of the Minnesota River and his life as a father, husband and public servant. Grandpa lived in an era when the country schoolhouses dotted the countryside. It was his job as county superintendent of schools to manage and oversee the operations of these small, but vital one room schoolhouses. There came a time when the schools had to consolidate. This meant the one room schoolhouses were to be closed down, the children were bused to bigger public schools and the teachers lost their jobs. As Grandpa talked of this, I could tell in his voice, how difficult this had been for him as he was put into the position of being the liaison to make this happen. Clearly, it had been a painful experience as he cared deeply for not only the teachers who served under him, but also for the students as they were uprooted and life as they knew it, was changed forever. One statement he made still rings clear for me today: "I always tried to get along with everyone." In his wisdom Grandpa knew in spite of whatever was happening, it was his job to be a servant of reconciliation. Was he perfect at it? Of course not. But he was an elected official and he knew his calling as a superintendent was to get along with people. Sometimes his decisions were unpopular and perhaps he did some questionable things, but even after the schoolhouses closed, he worked at reconciling the things that were not right. Even after he died I would meet people who would tell me how much they had respected him and knew him as a person who lived by a principle of simplicity to be a minister of reconciliation.

This has been a hard, hard principle for me to live by. The world says "It's not fair" and this phrase screams endlessly in our culture. And as the culture of our world tells me this it inwardly reinforces what I am already telling myself on an emotional level. Living with the attitude of unfairness makes life complicated and chaotic, especially when it comes to relationships. And that is usually where life gets most complicated. I am a restorative person and this is how I am wired; it is central in my life and what drives me. Of all the challenges I have had, being reconciled in relationships in my life has been the most difficult of all. It is far easier to restore a physical therapy patient than a broken relationship and as I coach my clients it is a reality that problems in relationships are usually complex and deep rooted.

The prefix "re" means again. Essentially reconciliation and restoration, means to begin again. As a restorative person I am the eternal optimist when it comes to hope for people. And it has been a hard lesson for me to understand that as a minister of reconciliation I need to do my part, but ultimately, it is God who will do the reconciling in His own way and in His own time. During my search and struggle with this I asked God "what do I do?" The big question was how I would reconcile myself to someone who screams "Life is not fair and I am angry and bitter and I want vengeance because of that!" And this is what God said to me: *"Heap burning coals upon their head."* What? Did I hear God right? Is this just folklore or is it biblical? I hope I heard Him right. And so my quest for where reconciliation begins took on new meaning. As I searched to make sure I was hearing God right I looked in my Bible. Heaping burning coals is so biblical that it is quoted in both the Old and New Testament (See Proverbs 25:22 and Romans 12:20). In other words, put an exclamation point on at the end of that command.

But what exactly do heaping burning coals mean? It sounds vindictive and painful. As I searched for the hidden meaning of this I learned what this was. (NIV Bible study notes) The Egyptian ritual was that when a person was repentant and wanted to be reconciled, he would carry a bag of glowing coals on his head. Another helpful fact to shed light on this is that hot coals were vitally important to the people. Hot coals were essential to keeping a fire going. If someone was carrying a pan of hot coals (it was customary to carry this on top of the head) and another person walked by with a tub of hotter coals, as a sign of kindness, the person with the hotter coals would add to the tub of coals that was at risk of burning out. In looking at the whole passage in Proverbs, God's command is simple. Return good for evil. The concept is a person can be brought to repentance by being kind to the person who has hurt them. Once there is a heart that is repentant, reconciliation can be possible. The desire for revenge needs to replaced with an attitude of kindness.

I know in your mind you may be struggling with this idea, because the heart is still saying, *"It's not fair!"* Whenever I would argue with God about things not being fair, He would say, *"Vengeance is mine."* In other words, His calling for me is to be a minister of reconciliation and to leave the rest up to Him. Showing kindness is not a guarantee the person you are attempting to reconcile with will be repentant. In fact, sometimes it may make the person angry. But in the end, you have done your part to be a minister of reconciliation and in your heart you can know you can move forward having done it with kindness. If you look closely at the passage in 2 Corinthians, you will see that it says, *"Christ reconciled himself to us."* He did the action and didn't wait for us to come to Him, thank goodness. He set the example and because He reconciled himself to us, He wants us to do the same in our own relationships. Since Jesus did the reconciling to us, is it too much for Him to ask us to do the same?

Who is one person you need to reconcile with in your life?

Have you reconciled yourself to God through repentance?

What does vengeance look like to you?

Do you find yourself heaping those burning coals by being outwardly kind, while inwardly gritting your teeth saying, "it's not fair?"

If Christ reconciled himself to us by dying for our sins on the cross, what is the least you can do to be a minister of reconciliation?

From the Great Reconciler

    My Servant, I have given you the ministry of reconciliation. I have asked you to serve in that way. I know how difficult it can be. Remember, my son Jesus, was spit upon, rejected, abandoned, betrayed and crucified. But my kindness has lead multitudes to repentance (Romans 2:4) I know life is not fair. But I urge you to leave vengeance to me. I long to see my world restored and my people living in love and kindness. And I know there are those who have hardness of heart and will not return kindness when kindness is shown. But do your part. Allow reconciliation to begin with you. Do not wait for others to come around. It may be too late before that happens. Do it in a way where my son Jesus is glorified and people can see His face in you. After all, He gave His own life so you could be reconciled to me. When you heap on burning coals of kindness, it is a way of taking up the cross. It is not a natural thing to do and it is only through the power of my Spirit that this can truly be done. But at the end of the day, you will be glad you were my servant. It will bring me honor and it will bring you dignity. Vengeance is indeed mine. Understanding this will in itself simplify your life. So through your genuine kindness the door is open to repentance and it is only then when a relationship can truly be restored. Through your kindness you become a person of integrity and respect. So rejoice in serving with me and for me by being my minister of reconciliation.

Being an Heir

*You are no longer a slave, but a son; and since you are a
son, God has made you also an heir.*
Galatians 4:7

Have you ever received an inheritance? I did, but it was sad and bittersweet. My receiving an inheritance came from a loss, and it happened when my parents died. I learned a huge lesson during that time: no amount of money can ever replace a person or the relationship with that person. I often said it after our family farm was sold and the money was dispersed that I would give it all back to have my parents with us again. How I longed for them to call me by name just one more time. My role as their daughter was shattered by death and the whole experience changed me forever. No longer were earthly things as important. It forced me to change my perspective on this earthly life. And in many ways I longed for life to be simple and free from loss and to just be a daughter again.

As you look at this verse in Galatians, spend some time reading the verses before it. Paul is writing a letter to the people in Galatia and it was his intent for them to see that as sons and daughters of God, they could go to their heavenly father anytime and say *"Daddy, Daddy!"* The original name used in the passage is *Abba, Abba* which is a personal term of endearment used much in the same way that we say *Daddy*. If one sentence could sum up what this passage is saying, it is this: we can receive the inheritance God wants us to have if we understand He is our father and giver of not only this earthly life but also the inheritance of eternal life.

I loved my dad and growing up on a farm we had great times together. I rode with him to town in the big old green truck and helped him with the chores and the animals. Later in life I learned that we relate to our heavenly father much in the same way we related to our earthly father. While I had a good relationship with my dad, he was not perfect. None of our earthly fathers are. Dad could be overprotective and a perfectionist at times. He wanted only the best for me, but because of his short comings as a human parent and me as a human daughter, there were times when our relationship suffered for it. Later, as a mother to my sons, I came to understand my own humanness even more and it has been a most humbling experience to be a parent to them.

Coming through the ups and downs of life and I desired to have a deeper and more intimate relationship with my heavenly Daddy. Part of this journey was in how God provided the opportunity for me to find healing in the areas where my earthly dad had fallen short. As I listened to a speaker at a conference on healing in the family, I began to understand my earthly viewpoint and the subconscious connection I made between my earthly and heavenly fathers. The tough part was my earthly father had long gone to heaven, so the healing would have to come from the work of the Holy Spirit, not from a conversation with my dad. Sitting in the conference for healing of the family I cried and cried and cried. The pain of years way back began to emerge and I was simply at a point where I had a choice and could let the pain fester and simmer and keep me from healing. Or, I could allow the Holy Spirit to do His deep healing work in my heart. I never knew the pain was so deep and so hidden. My dad had been such a good father, but there had been a rift in our relationship. The time came when we had to reconcile or forever be alienated from each other. This time came as he was in the hospital dying. I knew the horror stories others had about fathers who were evil and my dad had never treated me in a way to cause intentional harm.

In spite of reconciling with my dad before he died and in spite of my childhood being a good one, there was an unhealed corner of my heart and the Holy Spirit had some work to do in me. I heard that God, my heavenly dad, wanted me to enjoy the inheritance of His love while I was still on this earth. So I sat in this conference on healing for the family and worked through some intentional steps. This process brought a new understanding in what I was telling myself about my heavenly dad, based on how my relationship with my earthly dad had been. As a result of this Spirit-filled time I had one of the most profound healing experiences of my life. I learned my heavenly dad would never wrongly accuse me, abandon or reject me. There would never be a time when Heavenly Dad would say, *I can't or I won't help you.* And best of all, my heavenly dad would call me *"Daughter"* forever and forever and for all eternity!

As for the inheritance, I came to understand I am no longer a slave to anything that is not from God. The opposite of being a slave, is that I am His daughter. And if I am His daughter, I am entitled to an inheritance. The inheritance is not of the earthly stuff my earthly father left, but it is in His kingdom of heaven. It is important to remember the inheritance from our heavenly father is so easy to obtain compared to the complexities of getting an earthly inheritance.

I discovered and healed and came to know my heavenly and earthly Daddies were different from each other and there was healing available. I could enjoy the benefits of my heavenly inheritance while still here on this earth. Simplicity and living with a heart where the Holy Spirit could dwell made having the promise of receiving a heavenly inheritance such a magnificent blessing that all I could do was cry with joy and say, *"Abba, Abba!"* I still call out to my earthly dad at times. When I am stuck with a question about my trees (an interest we shared together) or when I wonder about a time from the past and would like to just talk to him about it I cry out, *"Dad, Dad."* The answers to my earthly questions will have to wait until I get to heaven. And then they won't matter anymore, just as the earthly inheritance won't matter either. But one thing I do know, my heavenly dad is calling out to me by name and wants me to be His daughter. He is saying to me "Jayne, I am your father and I welcome you into my arms. I am waiting for you in heaven and have your inheritance ready, but I am also available for you in place of your earthly dad."

In what ways do you see your earthly dad in relation to your heavenly dad?

This can be very painful and difficult, so take some time and ask for the Holy Spirit to speak to your heart.

If you could say one thing to your earthly dad, what would it be?

If you could say one thing to your heavenly dad, what would it be?

Forgiveness is at the core of being able to live in the simplicity of saying, "*Daddy, Daddy.*" What do you need to forgive in your earthly dad?

Are you ready to enjoy the inheritance from your heavenly dad by letting go of the humanness of your earthly dad?

From Father God

    My child, I long for you to call me "Daddy, your Abba Father." I will never leave you nor forsake you. I will not hurt you or turn from you. If only you knew how much I love you and I can't wait to give you your inheritance! I know about the humanness of your earthly father. As your heart cries out to me, let your tears flow like a river (Lamentations 2:18). But allow those tears to bring healing and restoration to your life. And then you can come to know that I am perfect and not like the dads on earth. Invite the Holy Spirit to do the deep healing work of forgiveness in your heart. Forgive your dad and while you are at it, forgive your mother and yourself and, if necessary, your siblings too. Don't let anything get in the way of being able to experience the love I have for you. As a sovereign father, I can do far more than any earthly father can. As you grow in your relationship with me you will come to understand all I intended for us to have when I formed you. So as you cry "Abba, Abba" in the most painful places of your heart, you will experience the calling of my Spirit and will be free to enjoy the simplicity of my eternal inheritance, something far more wonderful than any earthly inheritance would ever bring. As you cry "Abba, Abba" you will hear me answer back "my child, my son, my daughter! I love you more than you will ever know!"

Chosen

*You are a chosen people, a royal priesthood, a holy
nation, a people belonging to God, that you may declare
the praises to him who called you out of darkness into
his wonderful light.*
1 Peter 2:9

One of my favorite things to do as a gardener is to pick flowers and arrange in a vase to brighten the kitchen or dining room table. The first flowers I pick in the spring are the daffodils, crocuses and tulips. In the heart of summer, lilies, roses and other summer perennials produce a rainbow of colors bringing life into the house. Finally, the last flowers are chrysanthemums to add brilliance to the autumn colors before the winter sets in. I am always in awe of the textures, colors and intricate details of flowers and it gives me such pleasure to have them setting on the table to bring beauty and joy.

Picking flowers is healing and restorative for me, and yet, it is such a simple thing. I remember my boys picking dandelions in the yard and bringing them to me to put in a vase on the table. My heart would give a little leap of joy at this simple gesture of love. To be picked to bring joy and happiness; what a privilege, even if it was only a dandelion!

Our verse in 1 Peter is about how God chose us and describes our identity in Christ. Peter is writing about whom we are and what we are to be. It summarizes one of the principles of simplicity. *We are chosen by God!* God sees us as His living and precious stones as Peter writes in chapter 2. In the margin of my Bible I marked this passage, verses four through ten, as the basis for our identity. God has chosen us to be His people, and we belong to Him. What a wonderful thing, just as I choose the flowers to set on my table. We are chosen by God and we belong to Him!

I have known Jesus as my Savior for a long time. I made that decision as a teenager, but the decision is twofold. The second part took a long, long time for me to know and understand and ultimately to make a choice. This second part came to me as I sat in a healing service a couple of years after my divorce. I was making progress in my spiritual healing and there were times when I felt the love of Jesus' presence, but I still held Him at a distance. On this particular night as I sat in silence, allowing the Holy Spirit to wash over me, a still small voice said to me, *"Isn't it time we become friends?"* At that moment I knew Jesus was choosing me to be His friend. He wanted me for eternity, which is what salvation is all about, but He also wanted me to have a living and active relationship with Him while I am here on this earth, not just when I get to heaven. As I sat in this healing atmosphere, tears streaming down my cheeks, I thought about the hole in my heart that was being filled with the peace and presence of Jesus. It was a peace I had heard other lovers of Jesus describe. The restoration of our friendship as I experienced as a little girl, but lost through the storms of life, was once again a reality.

God chose us to be His people. That is the reason for sending His son, Jesus, to die and rise again. But what are we to do with that in return? The answer to this is simple: we are to choose Him! We are to choose him as Lord and Savior to redeem us from our sin. That is the basis of John 3:16. My own paraphrase is: *God loves us so much as his chosen people that he was willing to sacrifice His one and only beloved son to die for us. If we believe this in our hearts, not just in our minds, we will not suffer the consequences of our sin. We will live with God forever in eternity.* This is a simple promise of love and hope and eternal restoration and life!

But between now and eternity, God wants us to have a real and living relationship with him. He doesn't want us to just understand and accept the simple truth of salvation, but He wants us to choose him as our friend while here on this earth. Just as any human relationship needs to be nurtured for it to grow, so it is the same when it comes to our relationship with God. The night God asked me to become friends was His invitation to take our relationship to a whole new level. He didn't want me to hold Him away at arms length, but to embrace our relationship with both arms held out wide. He wanted the Bible to be His love letters to me. And He wanted me to have an open heart and ears to hear the things He was waiting to tell me the things any best friend would say.

If Jesus is whispering in your ear, *"Isn't it time we become friends?"* what are you telling Him?

Because God chose you for Himself, are you ready to choose Him as your Savior?

Do you accept Jesus and His death and resurrection as the way to eternal life in heaven?

Do you confess and repent of the sins that keep you from receiving Jesus as your Savior?

Do you see God as your friend and desire to be in a relationship that needs to be nurtured for it to grow?

Are you willing to be a part of His chosen people where you can grow in your understanding of His great love for you?

From the One who Chose You

    You are indeed a chosen people, a holy nation, a royal priesthood and indeed, you belong to me. I have chosen you to be that, not because of what you have or have not done, but because I sent a Savior in Jesus to do that for you (Romans 5:8). As He died on the cross for your sins, I want you to believe in the simple fact that if you believe this in your heart you will live in eternity with me. My friend, your identity is not based on who you are as a mere human being, but rather who you have become through Jesus. Since I have chosen you, I want you to choose and acknowledge me in your heart as the Lord of your life in heaven and here on earth (Deuteronomy 4:39). As you choose and repent of the sin that keeps you from loving me as well as others, you will come to understand what it is to be part of a chosen people, a holy nation and a royal priest hood. And now, as I whisper in your ear, "Isn't it time we become friends?" I am asking you to come into a relationship with me. I want you to experience the benefits of being in relationship. I want you to be able to talk to me, feel my presence, and come to me with your questions and problems. I want you to fully embrace our friendship, with all your heart and with arms held out wide. I have chosen you, just as you would choose a beautiful flower or a precious stone. I want you to be with me in eternity someday, but I want you to choose me as your friend for this time on earth. And so today I am whispering in your ear, "Choose me, choose me! Isn't it time we become friends?"

Final Thoughts on Simplicity

Take some time and re-read these truths and think about what these statements are saying to you personally as though God himself is whispering them in your ear.

Remember:

1) You are a child of God; your identity is in Christ.
2) You are significant in God's eyes.
3) You were created for a purpose while here on this earth.
4) Get rid of what is hindering you spiritually, emotionally and physically.
5) God will never abandon, reject or betray you.
6) You have a dwelling place in your heart for God.
7) Leave behind anything that is complicating your life.
8) Pick the fruits of the Spirit to live by.
9) You can choose to be an overcomer.
10) God knows your needs and desires better than you do.
11) Reconcile by showing kindness.
12) You are an heir through God, your heavenly father.
13) You have been chosen by God; have you chosen him to be your Lord and Savior?

SOLITUDE

Solitude

Solitude is something we all need and even crave at times. It is a blessing from God, and yet as you will discover, it may also be difficult. It can be difficult to experience, to put into practice as a discipline and it can even be experienced in the form of a wilderness time. Sometimes solitude is self imposed and at other times it comes from the result of life circumstances.

The Bible has much to say about solitude and as I experienced all of the above over the course of the years, God was once again teaching and preparing me for what he had planned. The biggest benefit coming from my times of solitude has been in developing a closeness and intimacy with God which could not have been accomplished any other way. I spent time getting to know myself. I spent time healing, emotionally and spiritually in a way that only our great God can do. I experienced many of the aspects of solitude in the same way the characters of the Bible did. Solitude goes along with simplicity. When the practices of simplicity are in place, enjoying the benefits of solitude is easier.

I hope that during this time of solitude you will experience a nearness to God you haven't before and that your relationship with him will grow and flourish. If your time of solitude is in the form of a wilderness experience, I hope your relationship with God will still grow, in spite of the surrounding circumstances or the situation. During this season, follow the same guidelines as you did for simplicity as outlined in the beginning of this book. Memorize, read, study, reflect, be honest with yourself, pray and let God speak to you. Ask for an outpouring from the Holy Spirit to restore you.

Enjoy this time of solitude and perhaps it will become a part of your life, where you crave times to be alone with the Lord in the framework of how He wants to minister to you. Solitude is necessary for restoration of the mind, will and emotions. So sneak away as Jesus often did. Come back restored and refreshed, ready to experience all that God has planned for His will and purpose. One final thought; if you feel guilty for taking time away to have a season of solitude from a situation or piece of life, discard that feeling. As you will see, even Jesus frequently went away to solitary places. He needed to do this and then we as earthly humans definitely need those times too.

Seeking in Solitude

*"For I know the plans I have for you," declares the Lord,
"plans to prosper you and not harm you, plans to give
you hope and a future."*
Jeremiah 29:11

This is a well known Bible verse and if you read it for what it says at face value you may think you will prosper! It is indeed an encouragement verse, but there is a whole lot more to it. This passage was given to the prophet Jeremiah by God as he was ministering and prophesying to the Israelites during their time of captivity in Babylon. This time of solitude was not something they wished for, but was the result of their disobedience, rebellion and hard heartedness. Jeremiah was writing these words in a letter to survivors and verse 12 needs to be included in the study of this passage. Read verse 12 and pay close attention as Jeremiah writes, "then God says through Jeremiah, you will seek and find me when you seek me with all your heart."

This popular Bible verse is definitely one of hope, but it is also saying there is a responsibility in it for us. Call upon God, come to Him and pray. Seek Him with all our hearts and then we will find Him. That is God's ultimate plan for us and for our future and it is where our only real hope can come from. Did the Israelites look at their time of captivity, exile and slavery as a time of isolation from God or as a time of seeking and finding Him? In studying this, one can believe that the time of captivity turned from isolation to solitude when they sought God with all their hearts. Solitude then becomes a heart matter.

I remember one particular Christmas when I had the opportunity to experience this exact thing first hand. I had been dreading Christmas Eve because I knew I was going to be all alone. I had grown up with Christmas Eve being an *event* when all four of my grandparents would come over after church. As a child it was always the highlight of my year, not just because of the Christmas gifts, but because then everybody would be together. In later years as an adult, my husband and I would go to church and have an intimate Christmas dinner together and a private gift exchange between the two of us. Even though it was a smaller affair than the ones I experienced as a child, it was still a most precious time for me. But on this particular Christmas Eve I was alone. My boys were grown and were elsewhere and the plan was to get together with extended family on Christmas Day. So I went to church alone, then came home, turned on the lights on the Christmas tree, lit the candles and put Christmas music on. I was alone and it was a defining time for me. I had a choice to make. I could remember this as a desert time in the captivity of isolation or I could allow this to be a night of worship when I could experience what Christmas is all about and turn it into an evening of solitude with God. Mary and Joseph were in the solitude of the stable with the baby Jesus and this was to be a special Christmas with just Him. After all, Christmas is not about gifts, food and family. It is about God coming to us in the form of a baby as part of His plan for us to prosper in eternity!

So my own plan and vision of happy family-filled Christmases was replaced by a Christmas of solitude with the One who made Christmas happen in the first place. This defining time for me was the beginning of experiencing times of solitude rather than the hardship and pain of feeling isolated from God and the people I love. As I would learn, it was how God would be able to reach me best. It was how He got my attention and how He would get me all to Himself. But my part would be to call to Him, and come into His presence and to talk to Him in prayer. As I sought Him with all my heart, I would find Him in the solitude of being alone with only Him. It wasn't a prosperous Christmas by worldly standards, but it was a magnificent and Holy Christmas. It was a prosperous time with Jesus and took hope for the future to a whole new level. What a sweet time!

Are you in a season of being alone or are you seeking time to be alone in solitude?

Are you loving being alone or are you rebelling against it?

Are you just wishing for God to show you the plan or are you following the steps He asked the Israelites to take in discovering His plan for you?

What is your heart saying to you that could turn isolation into a sweet time of solitude with God?

What steps do you need to take to have a season of solitude, regardless of the circumstances of your life?

God Declares to You,

I have a plan for you, just as I did for the rebellious Israelites. And my promises and commands as I spoke through Jeremiah are the same for you today. I want you to love me with all your heart and it is only in those times of solitude that the heart can really seek and find (Psalm 119:2). I am an all knowing God and I do know what I am doing. I know what you need and desire better than you do. I understand that busyness and the exile of isolation prevent solitude of the heart. I long for your attention and a time when we can be alone together. Because it is only in these times of solitude we can get to know each other. It is only during these times of solitude when I can minister to the heart that is seeking me. Call upon me, embrace this time and if a time of solitude is hard to find, call upon me for that time and I will provide. Hope and a future come only from me when you are ready to take those steps of seeking me with all your heart. Whether you are alone during those supposedly momentous times or are never alone to the point where you wish for it, my plan is the same for you. So turn isolation and exile into solitude and turn busyness into a time to slip away with me. Seek me with all your heart, come to me, call me, and talk to me. I am listening and waiting to help you prosper in ways you never imagined. It will not be prospering by worldly standards, but for eternal prosperity. When you seek me with all your heart it will bring hope for the future.

Peace in Solitude

*A heart at peace gives life to the body, but envy rots the
bones.*
Proverbs 14:30

I have worked in the healthcare field for decades, and yet it is
only in recent years I became aware that people who are at peace with
themselves, their loved ones and with God, are the ones who have
the best chance to heal physically. As I made this observation, I was
fascinated by what patients told me about their outlook on life and
on other people. This affirmed to me that physical, emotional and
spiritual wellness is so interconnected that it is impossible to separate
them entirely. Another important observation I made as I worked with
the very elderly population is the value of having times and seasons of
solitude.

What is the first word that comes to mind when you hear the word
solitude? For many, the word peace is what comes to mind. Looking
at this little Bible verse in Proverbs, a recipe for wellness is wrapped
up in it. The book of Proverbs is a great part of the Bible, wrapping
practical principles for daily living in with spiritual principles. The end
result is a book that provides insight and wisdom for living a spiritually,
emotionally and physically healthy life. A friend told me recently that
as she read the Book of Proverbs she was struck by the fact that it is
largely a book of do's and don'ts. I had to reflect on this for a bit and as
I read segments of this book I found it to be true. But then I thought
about how much of life is like that. When I go to the doctor I am given
guidelines and suggestions of do's and don'ts for my physical health. So
as I thought about this, I found Proverbs 14:30 to be a classic Proverb
for wellness. But the real question is, "What does this have to do with
solitude?"

I was in a session with my prayer minister, Carolyn. One of the blessings of these times was that she prayed for me ahead of time and occasionally she would receive an insight from God she could share with me in our session together. This verse from Proverbs is one she gave me and it came at a time when looking back, was the beginning of the time when God wanted to teach me about solitude and peace.

A heart at peace; how does a person find peace? What is a favorite thing to do to find this peace? For me, it means being in an intentional time and place of solitude. Solitude and peace go hand in hand. The physical place of peace and solitude is different for everyone. Perhaps it means sitting in a hot bath tub with the door locked. For another it might mean sitting on the front porch watching the sunset (that's me) and for another it might mean walking in a park or sitting on the lake in a boat fishing alone. For me, this verse was plainly saying if I wanted to have a heart of peace I must first find a physical place of solitude. Many times it is when a person is in a physical place of solitude that the secret places of the heart can be examined. This is where one can listen for the heart of God. I know, for some people the thought that may cross one's mind is *that's scary.* But perhaps that is why we have the other part of Proverbs, the part that says *"if you don't."*

Take another look at Proverbs 14:30. If a heart is not at peace, what happens? The next part says there will be rot. An example of the opposite of peace is envy. God knew my heart at this point when my prayer minister spoke this verse to me. And if there is one secret sin I struggle with (by the way, there is more than one) it is envy of others. I envy my friends who have been blessed in their marriages, who have had parents alive into old age, who work fun, flexible well paid jobs, etc. The day I received Proverbs 14:30 I was envious of my ex-husband who was living the life he wanted. Along with envy I was able to multiply how I was feeling and add other words that would describe my spiritual, emotional and physical condition. Some of these were:

The broken heart (Isaiah 61:1)
The heavy heart (Proverbs 25:20)
The troubled heart (John 14:27)
The anxious heart (Proverbs 12:25)
The grieving heart (Lamentations 2:18)

Because we have a God who specializes in restoring the heart, my times of solitude provided the time and space for Him to work through all of those unhealed areas including an envious heart that will rot the bones. As God met me in my heart through Carolyn, He continued to minister to me, and I came to know that He understood. The above list was gradually replaced with this list:

The singing heart (Psalm 30:11-12)
The rejoicing heart (1Samuael 2:1-2)
The secure heart (Proverbs 3:5)
The grateful heart (Colossians 3:16)

Have you found a time and place of solitude where you can be in touch with your heart?

In this time and place of solitude what is your heart saying to you?

Do you have a heart of anger, discouragement, deceit, greed or rebellion?

Or have you become hard hearted?

In searching for what God is saying to your heart, what are you replacing your unhealed heart with?

What is the heart of God saying that will restore you to Him, to others and to your own well-being?

Could your unhealed heart also affecting you emotionally or physically?

The Heart of God

    My love, I created you with a beating heart that is the core of life for your physical well being. It pumps the blood that provides life to you. And I created you with a heart of emotions, which gives you the ability to love, to feel, to know and understand. And I created you with a spiritual heart; the heart that connects with me, knows right from wrong, is unique to you as a human being and is not found in any other creature other than the human. Be alone with me and pour out your heart to me. I already know the condition of your heart, but I want you to know the condition of it. It is only when the human is in a place and time of solitude that the true condition of the heart can be revealed. If you desire wellness in your life, look at your heart and allow me to restore it. I created you as a three dimensional person and even though you may try to choose the parts you want restored, I know all parts need the miraculous healing power of my restorative love. I have given you the enduring power of my love letters in Scripture to know where my heart is for you. As you search your heart, search for me and my love in those love letters. As you are in a place and time of solitude, listen to the beating of your heart. Listen to what it is saying to you. And listen to what I am telling you. When you listen in solitude you will be amazed that it is not rottenness, but the wellspring of life I have in store for you. And as I write a love letter to you in Proverbs 4:20-23, follow what I am saying when I write. "Pay close attention to what I say; listen closely to my words, keep them in your heart for they are the life to those who find them and health to a man's whole body."

Enduring

For everything that was written in the past was written to teach us, so that through endurance and the encouragement of the Scriptures we might have hope.
Romans 15:4

In my roles as life coach, physical therapy clinician, mother and friend I am given countless opportunities to encourage people. Many times people need encouragement to, well, just simply endure. Modern day terms for this would be hanging in there, staying the course or persevering. But for how long and how much does one need to put up with? Where are the boundaries? When was the last time you had to persevere in a situation? You knew in your heart it was a matter of persevering because it was the right thing to do.

During a very difficult time of my life, when God had me in a season of solitude, I had to have a psychological evaluation done for a court proceeding. It was one of those scenarios where I felt like I was in a soap opera and repeatedly asked myself "How did I ever get here?" The reason I was required to under go this type of evaluation was the result of circumstances that were out of my control. My involvement in this *situation* was strictly by association. The only words I could find to describe the ordeal were weird, bizarre and out-of-body. Years later I can look back and say it was bad at the time, but today it no longer matters—not in the least! Most of us are faced at one time or another with circumstances in life that are *strange*. It may leave a person scratching one's head, shrugging the shoulders and saying "oh, well" and then resigning oneself to endure.

The results of the psychological evaluation showed that I am *normal*. But there was a statement in the report that stung, and even years later, I look at it as a form of persecution for my faith in Christ. It certainly is not to the extremes Paul endured as he traveled on his missionary journeys, spending time in jail for his outspoken faith in Christ. But nevertheless, written and spoken words sometimes sting and feel like a form of persecution. Because of my worldview and relationship as a believer in Christ and the life principles based on Him I try to apply in daily life, the psychologist labeled me as *moralistic*. I plainly remember, going to Webster's dictionary and looking up the word *moralistic*. At first I wasn't sure what the word meant and I had to read the meaning several times. The phrase jumped out at me: *extreme in spiritual and religious view points*. The report and the label I was given felt harsh, unfair and judgmental. In all my life, my Christian viewpoint and principles had never been so challenged. And probably the hardest thing of all was I was not given the opportunity to defend my stance or viewpoint. The report was complete and it had labeled me as a *religious extremist*.

Something else stands out for me as I look back at all of this. I distinctly remember sitting alone in solitude the evening after I read the report, trying to comprehend what I had said that would label me as an extremist. I was sitting on my front porch rocker alone watching the sunset as I do as often as possible. It was one of those brilliant, orange, hazy, late summer sunsets that slightly took my breath away because it was so magnificent. I watched many sunsets like this before, but on this evening it was as though God was telling me even though life seemed hazy from the *weirdness* of the situation at the time, he was there for me. It was a sunset of hope and encouragement, a sign to endure. This sunset was meant to be enjoyed alone in solitude, only in God's presence. As the sun slowly lowered, its rays fell on my face and it was as though God himself was touching me. Suddenly tears were streaming down my face. I knew even though I had been given a label because of my faith, I had said and done the right thing. I hated the *world* at that point, but knew I needed to endure and God would be there to provide for me.

That evening remains in my memory as one of the most poignant examples of being in solitude and experiencing a direct blessing from God. He didn't take the situation or the report away, but He provided a way for me to be able to endure. I have not changed my worldview or how I live my life. I don't think loving Jesus and trying to live life the way He did is really being an extremist. But I suppose it depends largely on how a person views Him. If that makes me extreme, then I don't mind enduring! What a blessing the solitude was!

What are you enduring? Is it an illness, a loss, a circumstance out of your control or is it simply because you are living here on earth?

Are you compromising, giving in or struggling with the whole idea of endurance?

Are you questioning whether you are in a place or position where you can continue to endure?

What is God telling you about endurance through the written words found in the Bible?

When was the last time you were in solitude, and knew God was was giving you hope and encouragement?

My Enduring Word

I am a God of endurance and I fully understand what it means to endure. Through my Spirit, my written word has endured for centuries. Neither war, nor collapse of empires or the forces of nature have destroyed my written word for you. I intend for those words to help you endure, to give you hope and encouragement. Remember what my son, Jesus, endured on the cross for you. Through my written word I gave you numerous examples of faithful people who endured for me, what I am and what I did for humankind. Through many of these people, it was in the time and place of solitude where I revealed myself to them. And that is why solitude is so important. It is a necessary thing if a person is to endure in me. As I am with you through my written word and my Spirit, take the time to be alone with me and let me encourage you and give you hope. Let my presence clear the haze and craziness the world tries to spin. And know in spite of insults and distorted world views and the evil that seems to be everywhere, there will be a sunset of endurance, a sign if you will, that I am present. Come to me alone and open yourself up to what I want to encourage you in. Keep a steadfast heart and when it is difficult for you to endure, remember my righteousness will endure (Psalm 112:7-9). The haze will clear and you will know that enduring the present will some day be but a memory of the past.

Refuge

He will cover you with his feathers, and under his wings
you will find refuge.
Psalm 91:4

I have been fascinated with birds since I was a little girl. I remember finding fledgling robins that had tumbled out of their nest as they learned to fly. I would pick one up, much to the mother's dismay and I would marvel at the softness of its feathers. I also remember finding various bird's nests tucked in among the bushes and trees. Many of these nests were lined with feathers from other birds that had shed theirs. It amazed me how in God's creation, nothing is wasted when it comes from Him.

Another fascination I had with feathers was when we would be fishing and the weather was cold and sometimes misty and rainy. And yet the ducks and Canadian geese didn't seem to mind as they swam on the lake, keeping a close eye on us at all times. They did not mind the cold water and in fact, even enjoyed it. Their feathers acted as a protective barrier to insulate them from the elements and the water would even form beads from the oil on their feathers. What a magnificent idea God had when he created the birds and fowl.

During my place and time of solitude I spent some time reading the Psalms. They became a favorite way for me to find comfort, peace and hope. I invite you to spend some time reflecting on them and you will discover for yourself the hope and encouragement they give. During my season of solitude there were a number of *life concepts* I spent a fair amount of time thinking about. Trust was one of those concepts and it took me years to fully comprehend what trust is all about. Some of the biggest lessons I learned was I could be in a place of safety and security with only God and I could just *be*. I did not have to say or do anything. One of the hardest lessons to learn about trust is the state of *being*. The state of *being* can be challenging at times, especially for someone like me who is fairly driven and goal oriented. But little by little, I learned it is important to find times of solitude because it is only then I can experience *being* in the refuge of God's presence fully and completely.

During my difficult times I can take refuge in solitude and come under the wings of God's protection and provision. He can cover me with His *feathers* and I can rest in peace and solitude. Psalm 91 is a classic piece of God's promises for those who trust in Him. As I read and highlighted the sentences in this Psalm it affirmed God's protection over me. I was struck by imagery of just what and who God is protecting us from. For me, sometimes that means God is protecting me from myself.

A good example of this can be explained by a dream my mom had one night. I don't remember exactly when it was, but I am sure it was about the time I was a *fledgling leaving the nest* or perhaps was *falling out of the nest* before I was ready to *fly*. She dreamt I was running around in the palm of a big hand. I was running fast and frantically and at certain times would get precariously close to the edge of the hand, nearly falling out of it. But just as I was about to plunge, the hand would fold in ever so slightly, bringing me towards the center and back to the center of security again. My mom came to understand I was in the security and safety of God's hand and He would protect me from everything, including myself. She was given comfort through the dream that being in the solitude and security of God's hand, He would protect me and would keep me from falling.

That dream of refuge and safety my mom had was a lifetime ago. At the time, she had no idea as to what my future held. She was not with me to endure the trials and challenges I would face later on. She knew me well, but didn't have insight about the good and the bad decisions I would make. But as a mother who had an ambitious and strong willed daughter, she knew God would need to keep me in the protective palm of His hand to save me from myself. Just as importantly, God knew she needed the reassurance He would protect me and she could release me to His care. He knew her heart and her desire. He would be there for me to come to for a place of refuge and solitude.

As you read Psalm 91, what snares, terror and arrows are you being protected from?

During this time of solitude, what is God telling you about His protection?

Are you able to *be,* resting under the safety of His *feathers* and in the refuge of His wings?

What is keeping you from trusting God to protect you?

Read Psalm 91 in its entirety, underlining all the promises of protection. Review these questions again, asking God to give you insight and wisdom about being in a place of refuge called *the solitude of safety under God's wing.*

A Place of Refuge

My precious little one, I want you to come under the safety and protection of my wings. Come into the solitude of love and trust that comes from experiencing my ongoing protection. I offer you a place of refuge where you can come and be. You do not have to do a thing, just be with me. Your soul can take refuge in me (Psalm 57:1). The fowler's snare and deadly pestilence may be lingering close by, but I am offering you myself as your refuge and fortress. Just as fledglings have a refuge and find solitude under the safety of the feathered wings of their mother, so do you have that same protection in me. My faithfulness is your shield, just as the water fowl have a shield in their feathers. You are under the protection of my love and the terror of the night, and the arrows of the day will not harm you. I will be with you when you are in trouble and I will deliver you. I have promised you that. So in this place and time of solitude, know that you are in a refuge of protection and you can trust me to cover you with my wings. The refuge of solitude is a place of safety. When you are in relationship with me you can learn to trust me and allow me to cover you with my wings. Enter into the refuge of my protection and rest beneath my wings.

Gaining Perspective

*Jesus, knowing that they intended to come and make him
king by force, withdrew again to a mountaintop by himself.*
John 6:15

It may seem a little ridiculous to memorize a Bible verse such as
this, but there is a reason for why I chose this one. This is a perfect
example of what Jesus did to separate Himself from *the world* when
life got to be too much. Jesus was faced with constant criticism as He
ministered to the Jews and Gentiles. His *life* challenges were different
form yours and mine, but nevertheless, even Jesus needed to take a
break now and then. When Jesus went into solitude He was able to
gain perspective and gather His thoughts and emotions. I believe John
intentionally included this observation about Jesus to impress on his
readers that what Jesus endured was not easy and wanted this to be an
example of what we as humans periodically need to do.

One of the blessings I have experienced in recent years has been
taking the time to go on a hermitage retreat. The retreat center I stay at
is on a beautiful parcel of woodland and prairie in central Minnesota.
The cabins or hermitages are designed to be simple, quiet and yet very
comfortable. Most of the time when I go on one of these retreats I spend
about half of the time just sleeping! I think this is because sometimes I
get to the point of exhaustion and don't even know it until I step away.
I go to the hermitage to rest, gain perspective, talk with God and be
restored to face whatever life is going to throw at me next.

A good example of one of these times was right after my dear
friend and prayer partner, Lois, died. At the same time my ex-husband
remarried, giving me the final answer to the passionate prayer that
restoration of my marriage was not going to happen. Along with all of
this, my coaching practice was not developing in the way I expected.

Financial pressures continued to mount and life in general was totally overwhelming.

So on a spectacular October weekend when the autumn leaves were at their peak of brilliance, I headed to my hermitage to rest and gain perspective. It may be true that I live in a beautiful wooded setting, most of the time alone, but at home there is always something needing to be done. The pile of bills stares me in the face, the phone rings just when I want to sit down, and I always have a to-do list of household chores or coaching things. It can be a challenge to just sit down, let alone try to gain perspective on life.

If you look at John 6 again, there are some things to note. Perhaps Jesus was facing the same type of challenges First of all, Jesus was just coming off of an intense time of ministry. He had demonstrated the miracle of the feeding the five thousand. We also see He had completed many miracles of healing and had been teaching thousands of people. He was mentoring and preparing His disciples for their future ministries. To top it all off, He was battling the misconception that He was the next deliverer for the Jews who were under the oppressive rule of the Romans. Even though Jesus was divine in nature, and in this respect could handle anything, He was also human. Even Jesus needed to get away by Himself sometimes.

Another point John made was that he said Jesus did this *again,* indicating this was a regular thing Jesus did. In other words, He made it a habit and a regular part of His life to go away by Himself. The final thing to take notice of in John 6:15 is that Jesus went to a mountaintop. I would have to say whenever I go away on a hermitage retreat it is a mountaintop experience for me. Oh sure, I sleep a lot, but I always hear from God, He gives me opportunities to witness His miracles of nature firsthand and I gain perspective on my relationships, career and life in general. I think there is a bit of symbolism in this passage in John. When he writes that Jesus went to a mountaintop, I can visualize Him finding a place to rest at the top of a mountain (which by the way would be a big hill by many standards). He would look out over the landscape with the Sea of Galilee below Him. Physically, emotionally and spiritually He could gain perspective of the circumstances He was dealing with. As Jesus looked down from the mountain He could take a broad look at the rugged, yet beautiful, terrain of the region. I would think the hard, rocky terrain didn't look quite as difficult from this view point. He could sleep and breathe in the fresh air putting His thoughts in order so He could deal with people again, including His own disciples. Jesus could spend time with His father, talk with Him, find direction and guidance and rest in the assurance His heavenly father was right there with Him.

I have come to love the times of solitude—of being totally alone. I always look forward to going away to the hermitage retreat center, but there are some things I also observed about this. Life tries to get in the way just before I leave. Usually a commitment comes up and I need to decide which is more important. Or an unexpected *event* happens, forcing me to adjust and prioritize what is most necessary to squeeze in before I can get away. A recent example of this happened this spring. After I made my reservation at the hermitage center, the father of a friend of mine died and the funeral was planned to be during the time I was to be on the hermitage retreat.

Another observation is the less I take with, the better. Every time I go, I take less with me than I did the time before. The center supplies me with all my needs and what I take with me would fall into the category of *desires*. I find desires sometimes clutter my ability to gain perspective and I learned less is better when it comes to solitude. Here is one small example. The last time I went I didn't take any reading material with me except for my Bible. On previous occasions I took my devotion book or another book I was reading at the time. I found if I truly wanted to hear from God, all I needed was His Word. Even though the hermitage center is not on a mountain, spending time alone with God is a mountaintop experience. Jesus knew what to do when life got to be too much and what He did is a good example for us. It is important to remember God wants us to be replenished and restored. My times of solitude have proven to be a mountaintop experience every time. I treasure those times and my perspective of solitude has been forever changed because of it. What a beautiful example of the blessings that come from this time of solitude.

Have you ever gone *away* by yourself for a period of time?

What emotional, physical and spiritual aspects of your life need to be brought into perspective? Perhaps it is difficult to even begin to answer this question.

What does a mountaintop experience look like to you?

What step do you need to take to have a mountaintop experience where you can gain perspective?

Take time to search the Scriptures and make observations as to where Jesus went and what He did for an intentional time of solitude. Write these times down to remember as an example.

I Invite You

I am holding my hand out to you, my Faithful One, and I invite you to come away with me. Leave everything behind you. Leave all that is physical where it is. Put all that is emotional away for now. And even all that is spiritual can wait until another time. I want you to go to the mountain for a time, just as my son, Jesus, had to do time and time again. It is only in a time away from everyone and everything else that I can truly minister to you. I will give you all you need. If it is sleep, I will provide it for you. If it is a time to cry, I will wipe away your tears. If it is the need for a mountaintop experience with me, you will not be disappointed. Jesus went away by Himself when He was exhausted. When the miracles and the malicious rumors and the hard work of ministry got overwhelming, He retreated by Himself. You may say be saying "I am already by myself." Then I will tell you that you are in a place of solitude many would envy. All you need to do is close your eyes and rest. Let me minister to you and help you gain perspective. Look at your life from the mountaintop. Listen and experience my words of renewal and restoration. Allow me to minister to you through My Word. Be refreshed and restored. I will restore your heart and soul (Psalm 23). You will need a wise heart and perspective that will help you so you can minister to others (Proverbs 10:8). It is only then you can go on, living the way I intended for you.

Sovereignty

But while Joseph was there in prison, the Lord was with him; he showed him kindness and granted him favor in the eyes of the prison warden.
Genesis 39:20-21

The Old Testament character, Joseph, happens to be one of my heroes. Read Genesis 37-46 for the whole story. Joseph was a spoiled favorite son of Jacob. Joseph's jealous brothers sold him into slavery, where he was betrayed by Potiphar's wife and by no fault of his own ended up in jail. As a young man, he is portrayed as spoiled and rubbed his favoritism into his brothers. In Egypt, as a slave, his integrity (as he showed by not sleeping with the king's wife) got him into trouble. But here is what the passage says, *"the Lord showed him kindness and favor."*

Joseph was in the solitude of prison. He was not there by his own doing. In fact, he did the right thing. But because of the evil nature of Potiphar's wife, she tried to get even with Joseph, taking revenge and having him thrown into prison. It is a classic, biblical example of good versus evil. So here we have Joseph in solitude for something that was not his fault. Does this sound familiar? Have you ever been betrayed and it left you feeling alone and forgotten? There was not a thing you could have done to prevent the situation and there was not a thing you can do to get out of it. This is exactly where Joseph was. And yet, pay special attention because the writer says the Lord was with him! And the writer explains how: *"He showed him kindness and granted him favor in the eyes of the prison warden."*

This passage is the perfect example of God's sovereignty. Yes, a bad thing happened and certainly God could have intervened and stopped the bad stuff at any point. The course of history could have been altered and this part of Genesis would have been written with an entirely different storyline. Joseph should have never gone to prison.

He should have never experienced this type of isolation and solitude. The story could have been different, but it wasn't. This is not what God had planned. Sound familiar in your own life? It certainly is the case in mine.

There are a number of examples in my own life where betrayal, abandonment, rejection and isolation left me thinking "How did I get here?" During those times I would say to myself, "How will I ever get out of this?" What is going to happen?" "Where are you, God?" "I don't like being alone!" "This is not fair." It happened to me in my relationships with my family, my work and yes, even my church. The events of good versus evil in each of these times left me feeling isolated and landed me in *a season of solitude*.

Some years back, my husband and I were removed from our church's roles. In the letter we received, we were removed because of circumstantial evidence. I remember reading the letter and my mind surging into a state of numbness. I had just remarried and it was supposed to be a happy time in my life. I knew the church to which we belonged was not emotionally or spiritually healthy, but being the restorative person I am, hoped and prayed somehow God would intervene. Instead the opposite happened. Reeling in the sting of rejection from my pastor, who knew, but did not believe my story, I struggled with the immediate feeling of isolation. But this is where God's sovereignty came in. People rallied around us. The pastor who married us also ministered to us. My husband and I took time to confess the sins we had committed, even though they had no bearing on the circumstances (much like Joseph's early arrogance had no bearing on his being thrown into jail).

And so we entered into a time of solitude. We were without a permanent church home and initially it seemed as though God didn't care. But he was right there with us. To prove it, God demonstrated his kindness to us. Looking back I can see the blessings we were given. Financially, we were blessed more so than at any other time in our lives. Friendships thrived and were even fortified. We were happy in our marriage. And we found a place to attend church. During this time of solitude the biggest blessing and plan was God was growing in me a heart for working with people who have been abused, rejected and abandoned. Through the experience of being removed from a church I developed empathy and a heart for others who have experienced the pain and hurt of rejection and abandonment.

Over the years I have met so many people who were hurt by others and it was an eye opener for me when I experienced and learned about spiritual abuse. Because of God's sovereignty in my life, I was able to experience solitude instead of isolation. In return, God has given me countless opportunities to minister to others who have experienced similar hurts. God did indeed show up during my time of solitude. And yes, He could have changed the course of events in my own life at any moment. But where would I be today? Would I be an effective minister for him? Would I be able to coach those who want to take steps forward in their lives? Would I be able to be an encourager in a world where there is such a lack of hope? I think not. In the end, God had His way. The church I was removed from closed and it was reborn under a new name. I don't know where the pastor is who had us removed. It no longer matters. What matters is God uses times of isolation to put us in a position of experiencing His favor and kindness. And that is the difference between isolation and solitude.

What circumstances have you been faced with that caused *Potiphar's wife to put you into jail?*

Are you feeling locked in isolation or can you accept your life as a time of solitude?

What is a possible hidden blessing you can take from your experience where God will use it for His purpose in the future?

If you could change the outcome and God had intervened at another point how would your life be today?

What step can you take that would be in alignment with how God has used his sovereignty?

My Sovereignty

Yes, yes, I am here with you. I know you think of your life as being isolated. I know your current imprisonment feels like isolation. I understand you think that I am not near by and evil has won out. But I have a plan. Time and time again I demonstrated this through my people in the Old and New Testaments. I put those people in the Scripture to give you hope and encouragement. Just as Joseph did, I want you to learn from them, draw hope and to see how I was faithful in showing favor and kindness. I ask you to take from your experience the opportunity to experience solitude. Expect my favor and kindness during this time. I am a sovereign God and my thoughts are not your thoughts, neither are your ways my ways, as I declared in Isaiah (Isaiah55:8). As you set aside trying to comprehend my ways, turn your heart toward singing with gratitude (Colossians 3:12). Rest in the fact through my favor and kindness I will give you blessings to use in the future. Be in solitude, not isolation, for this is a matter of perspective. It is during a time of solitude one can witness my sovereignty. And it is during solitude you will know me more so than if your life had gone differently.

Not Wasted

*Forget the former things; do not dwell on the past. See
I am doing a new thing! Now it springs up: do you not
perceive it? I am making a way in the desert and streams
in the wasteland.*
Isaiah 43:18-19

Webster's dictionary defines solitude as this, "The quality or state of being alone or remote from society." The past few days have been just that for me. In part this has been by choice. But there have been times when I have been alone and it was not by choice. When my marriage ended I entered into the darkest desert time of my life. The losses piled up. My life coach, Patty, told me a few years later as we discussed this that my grief list was *off the charts*. Yes, loss brought the desert time. This desert time was not self-imposed solitude. Divorce brought aloneness. Socially, my friends changed as the friends were *divided up*. Financially I was no longer secure with the division of two incomes, and spiritually I went into a time where I did not trust God. I was angry at Him for allowing this to happen.

I struggled with isolation, but God in His infinite patience, would continue to be faithful to me and continually provided streams of blessings in spite of the apparent hardships. However, I continued to struggle with the past and the more I was alone, the more I perseverated on what had happened. The only reprieve I could find from the pain of the past was through work and going to school. Somehow, I knew I needed to learn to embrace the aloneness and to change my perception of it. I knew God had me in a time and place of being alone so He could accomplish in me what He intended. I read, prayed, searched, cried and yelled at God. Sometimes a friend would call and I would *dump* all my stuff. I experienced the absolute lowest depth of loneliness taking me into the desert of depression; one that I couldn't get out of without outside help. It seemed as though whenever I would experience *a stream in the desert* I would end up back in the *wasteland* again.

Solitude can be a good thing or it can be a bad thing, depending on how a person perceives it. We see numerous biblical examples of this. Joseph (Genesis 39), Daniel (Daniel 6), and Paul (Acts 16) were in the solitude of prison and yet their perception was not of being alone, but rather in the place where God could work through them. I was getting stuck. I was not allowing the Holy Spirit to take charge. Yes, part of grief is the stage of depression. But I was cycling through and not taking steps to move forward. I was using the time of solitude to cycle back through events and circumstances in my life that brought me to this point. I understood my identity in Christ, my purpose for living and that I am significant in God's eyes. Why then was I alone?

My intentional exercise the past few days has been to experience solitude in a way that is not a desert time, but rather a time in which I can truly experience God. As I sat on my porch last night I reflected on this. It was a beautiful summer evening. There was no moon and the stars had the sky all to themselves. They were shining in all their glory, millions of them at various stages of brightness. It was quiet except for the occasional hoot of an owl or the howling of the coyotes. There I sat, just God and me. The whole day had been that way. My boys called briefly as they often do, but other than that there had been no other contact with the outside world. It had been a day of writing and reflection. Household chores were under control and my physical exercise for the day had been mowing the lawn and doing a few odd gardening chores.

So what made yesterday different from other summer days in recent years? It was that I *intentionally* made yesterday a time to be by the stream. Once again, I discovered it is a matter of perception. Yesterday was different because I acted on this perception. I have known for awhile that God intentionally allowed me to be alone in this time and place, but yesterday was the day I also experienced it in my heart. My purpose was to write, which only works when I am alone. I also had the blessing of spending time alone with God. Instead of spending so much time thinking about summer weekends of the past, I took the time to praise God, for that is all He wants from me.

In thinking about the circumstances of recent years and looking back, I have very few regrets. The one regret I have is I let aloneness, depression, despair and the desert time rob me of a time many people would absolutely envy. I distinctly remember a time when I wished for the opportunity to have time alone. Perhaps you are on that end of solitude, but the only chance you get to be alone is in the car on the way to work, or a few minutes at the end of the day after everyone else is in bed. At that point you are too exhausted to truly experience the blessing of solitude. Perhaps your own personal desert is being locked into cares, commitments and the trials of living in our society and fallen world. At this point, you crave *the water of a calming stream* to give you the fortitude to press on. I have been in that desert too. It is all the more reason to take an intentional time for solitude and to make it not just a mind thing, but also a heart thing.

I sat alone with God last night, reflecting on solitude. As I am writing this I am struck with how Isaiah was prophesying not only to the Israelites, but also to me, even to the point of describing the creatures of nature such as owls and jackals who found water in the desert. As I sat on my porch, enjoying the streams of water through God's presence I believe the coyotes and owls, awake in the darkness, were also honoring God in their solitude.

Is solitude a waste of time to you, a time in the wasteland of the desert or a time when your mind and heart can connect with God?

Do you spend your time in solitude mulling over things of the past or can you see God doing a new thing?

What change do you need to make to intentionally experience solitude as a stream in the wasteland?

Reflect not only the verse from this reflection, but also on the entire passage in Isaiah. What correlations can you make with your own desert time and the times when God provides streams in the wasteland?

Jayne Kane

From God through Isaiah

    I am commanding you to stop dwelling on the past. This is not what I intended for your time of solitude. I know I have given you a memory so you may enjoy the good ones and learn hard lessons of the bad ones. During this time of being alone, whether it is self imposed or by my ordination, use this solitude to praise me with all your heart (Psalm 9:1). As you experience blessings from water of the streams, you will have an outpouring of the Holy Spirit. I understand the desert as I created it and I understand the spiritual and emotional desert you find yourself in. But rest assured through your personal decision to make the desert a time of solitude that focuses on praising me, you will experience blessings of why I chose you. I said it twice through Isaiah. I am the one who provides water in the desert and streams in the wasteland. I am the one who provides water for my creatures and they honor me for it. I am the one who provides the water for you in the wasteland of solitude. I formed you for myself so you can praise me and be with me. Rest assured, in this time of solitude whether it be a time of aloneness or a time of rest, I have formed you for myself. All I desire from you is to see that I am doing a new thing. I know it is only through the desert of solitude I can make this new thing spring up. Trust me; there is no wasteland when you are praising me! Even the owls and the coyotes of the night know and honor me for it!

Encountering God

So Jacob was left alone, and a man wrestled with him
until daybreak.
Genesis 32:24

This verse may seem a little strange verse to memorize and reflect on. If you read the entire story surrounding this verse, you may gain a new understanding of what can be gained in a time or season of solitude. I learned this story as a child in Sunday school along with another story about Jacob that parallels it (see Genesis 28:10-22). A similarity for Jacob in both Genesis chapter 28 and chapter 32 is that Jacob is alone. Neither Father Abraham, nor Brother Esau is mentioned in either of these stories. Both of these times Jacob had one-on-one encounters with God. But the difference in the two stories is that in Jacob's dream, God came in the form of an angel. In the wrestling match God came in the form of a man.

During my times of extended solitude, I struggled and wrestled with God many times. I know through many tears and the groaning of my heart and my constant asking "God, why is this happening to me?" I was wrestling with Him. There were many times when I was angry at God for not fixing my life. I wanted the struggle to be over and I wanted to be blessed! But God wanted something else for me. He wanted me to get to know Him more deeply and more intimately.

Wrestling is the oldest sport in the world. If you have ever watched it, it is easy to conclude there is no other sport that has as much physical contact as wrestling. As we look at this story of Jacob wrestling with God take note of a couple of things. Jacob sends his family across a stream and stays back to be alone. He is physically separating himself from his family and possessions. He went to a place of solitude, physically separated and set apart for this time. This was not new to Jacob as he was used to being alone and separated. He was a shepherd by trade and many times in this type of livelihood it was just the shepherd and his flock.

Jacob struggled at other times in his life, trying to prevail—first with Esau and then with Laban (Genesis 27). But as Jacob was traveling with his family and about to re-enter the promised land of Canaan, this was different. As Jacob wrestled with this man through the night, there came a point where they stopped and had a face to face meeting. At the end of this encounter, the man blessed Jacob. Jacob knew he met God face to face, which is why he named the meeting place "Peniel" (Genesis 32:30). The story ends with the sun rising on a new day, but Jacob ends up with a chronic limp from the wrestling match. The best part of this story is that Jacob had a new understanding of God. He knew God could have overpowered him. Instead, in the place of solitude called "Peniel" God showed mercy and blessed Jacob for his persistence.

Most of my times of solitude and wrestling with God happened as I worked in my gardens. As I worked alone, planting, weeding and pruning, I struggled with God about my life and how the course of events had not gone my way. I reminded myself that I asked to get to know Him more deeply and more intimately and there is no better way to get to know someone than through a face to face encounter. Season after season I struggled with God about situations in my life. Recently I read through some of my notebooks where I wrote about the struggles. The funny thing is, the struggles of the past are no longer struggles today. As I wrestled with God alone in solitude and asked Him to take the problem away, God did. He blessed me, just as He did for Jacob.

The best part of my encounter with God came *after* the struggle and times of wrestling with Him. God's truth and direction came through His Word and sometimes He put a godly person in my path to minister to me. He used a variety of ways to give direction, sometimes coming through a book or from a word of wisdom. Other times God gave me a word to reveal Himself to me through an aspect of nature or creation. Through all those times and through all the ordeals in my life, God spared me. He could have overtaken me. Instead He blessed me for my persistence in struggling with Him, just as the case was with Jacob. To truly have a face to face, one on one encounter with God, a person needs to be alone in solitude.

Jacob did indeed end up with a permanent limp after his encounter with God. All of us have limps and other permanent scars from our past struggles. It becomes a minor inconvenience when put into the right perspective. To stay with God through the struggle and persist in the face to face encounter will bring blessings. Jacob was blessed by having a great nation, Israel, named after him. If I gave a name to my gardens I would probably name them "Peniel" because I too, had an encounter, a struggle with God, alone in solitude, face to face at home.

Have you had an encounter with God recently?

What struggles, arguments, wrestling matches and other difficulties have you taken up with God?

Who won?

Jacob was blessed for his persistence. Are you being persistent with God or are you giving into fear, discouragement and bitterness?

For some people, having an encounter with God can be scary and intimidating. Is it for you?

If so what are you trying to hide?

Do you have a limp or another scar that is a reminder of your struggle with God?

Jacob was blessed by having a great nation named after him. What is the possible blessing God would like you to experience from your time of struggling in solitude?

How would God like you to use that great blessing for His glory?

Meeting Me

    Walk across the stream and be alone in solitude with me. Bring your struggles, your frustrations, your hurt, pain and even your anger. During the nighttime as you wrestle with questions, conflicts, difficult situations and people, know I am in the struggle with you. As you come through this, become an overcomer, just as my son Jacob was. But you need to know to be an overcomer, you need to see me face to face. It may be in the form of a man or other earthly way that I so often use. But it is only through getting to know me intimately, face to face, that you will in the end be truly blessed. In your time and place of solitude I can overtake you at any point. I am God. But it is my desire that you will know me intimately and I desire to bless you through that. I will spare you and there will be a new day. I hear the groaning of your broken heart (Ezekiel 21: 6) and in the end there may be a limp or other scar, but that will be far outweighed by the blessing that comes only from seeing me face to face. Peniel was indeed a place were a struggle happened, but more importantly it was a place of solitude where I spared Jacob and blessed him. Find a place of solitude where you can struggle with me. Through your intimate time alone with me you will be blessed and in the end you too, will know that you were spared and will call it Peniel: a place of solitude where you saw me face to face.

Finding Clarity

But Jesus often withdrew to lonely places and prayed.
Luke 5:16

This verse gives a little insight into what Jesus did to restore Himself so He could continue doing ministry. Jesus was indeed divine in nature, but as a human being He needed to step away and find perspective and clarity. As a life coach, one of my roles is to help my client find perspective and it can be an interesting process. Once a perspective is gained, everything becomes clearer. Interestingly, quite often my client just needs to step back from the situation to find perspective and clarity.

There are four points I want to make from this short verse. The first one is Jesus did this often. It is not clear what often means. But if you see where the verse is placed in Luke's writing, you will notice it is sandwiched between doing miracles and teaching. These were the core of Jesus' ministry and as you read through the Gospels you will see that as Jesus was not only doing the hard work of teaching and miracle working, He was also frequently attacked on a variety of fronts. Ministry in itself was draining, but to constantly be under scrutiny and criticism made it even more difficult.

Another point to take from this verse is that Jesus withdrew. He simply slipped away by Himself with no announcement or fanfare. There was no agenda to it. It also struck me that none of the gospel writers who wrote about Jesus' times of solitude ever put them into a time frame of weeks, days or hours. It is just simply stated as a fact and was a part of how Jesus did life.

The third point in this verse is that He went to lonely places. For anyone who has struggled with aloneness and loneliness, this can be difficult to understand. Why go to lonely places and just what are lonely places? I would have to think this means He went to places where there weren't any comforts, even as they knew comfort of that time. He didn't withdraw to go on a vacation and the writers don't even say that He did it to restore his body, mind, and spirit, (although those could have been benefits of being in solitude). But to go to lonely places meant He was free of distractions.

Jesus went to the lonely places to pray, which is the fourth point. Jesus spent time in solitude to be with His Father. He went away to be alone and to talk to His Heavenly Dad and it was only then that Jesus could to talk to God one on one. It was then He could regain perspective and clarity. As Jesus did this He was able to continue in His role, mission, vision and purpose for His earthly ministry. Conversing with God alone would give Jesus whatever He needed to withstand the attacks of the Pharisees as well as multitudes of others who would come up against Him.

One of our favorite things to do as a family when my boys were growing up was to go camping in northern Minnesota. Our first trips were to campgrounds with the comforts of showers, bathrooms, clean drinking water and firewood nearby. Gradually we got more adventurous and we boated to remote islands along the Canadian border. I can remember lying in the tent at night listening to the howl of the timber wolf. It is a lonely and even somewhat eerie sound. Of course, my husband and boys were nearby, but nevertheless, the lonely cry of the timber wolf painted a vivid image in my mind of the loneliness of these animals. I would think about how lonely the remote island we were staying on would be if it was just me there alone. It was on these trips my husband and sons would go off fishing and leave me alone (but safe). I would sit perched on a big rock overlooking the lake and I would soak in the scenery. It did indeed bring clarity to my relationships, my purpose and my life.

Vacations like that were restorative to the body, mind and spirit. I would go back home and the everyday things didn't seem like as much drudgery. I felt as though I could get through just about anything life threw at me and I had new appreciation for the things I often took for granted. Going away to a lonely place became a sort of spiritual discipline. Perhaps the one lesson I learned about solitude in loneliness is this: lonely times and places are not lonely if you spend it with God.

When was the last time you took a sabbatical and spent time alone without the distractions or the luxuries of our culture?

Do you find it restful or anxiety producing to be alone without an agenda or timeframe?

Is your prayer time with God a conversation or simply meditation on self?

What step do you need to take to bring clarity to your life?

Your ministry?

Your relationships?

Your future plans?

Our Conversation

Withdraw to the place of loneliness, my servant so you can be with me and talk to me. Put aside your agenda, your watch, your timeframe and your work. The demands of the world are too much for anyone to constantly come up against without taking time to withdraw and talk to me. Come and pray and enter into conversation with me. Let me minister to you and bring clarity to whatever is bogging you down. My son, Jesus was an example of how to restore the body, mind and spirit as He often slipped away to pray and be with me. Consider taking a sabbatical as a gift, not as an obligation or just another thing to do. Do it without expectations or self-imposed requirements. I know for some, solitude is more difficult than for others. But to be an effective servant of mine, it is a necessity, not a luxury. As you spend time in the lonely place, let your guard down. Be alone to get to know yourself and to get to know me more intimately. Leave the luxuries behind, for they only cloud reality. Pray and expect to hear from me. May the words of your mouth and the meditations of your heart be pleasing (Psalm 19:14) as you come from the place of loneliness in solitude. Serving is hard work, but you will find your effectiveness will be re-energized when you step back into reality. Clarity brings wisdom. It is with true wisdom coming only from me that you can serve me the way I intended.

Rebelling

Jonah went out and sat down at a place east of the city.
There he made himself a shelter, sat in its shade and
waited to see what would happen to the city.
Jonah 4:5

The story of Jonah is another one or those stories that many of us learn about in Sunday school. Usually the focus of the story is on the fact that Jonah ends up inside a whale when he goes against God's will. I recently participated in a Bible study on this popular book and when it was all said and done I had an entirely new viewpoint of Jonah. There was a concept that stood out for me and it is this: more important than the fact Jonah got swallowed up by a whale and went to Nineveh to prophecy to the people, is what happened afterwards. Pay special attention to this: after God spared Jonah and the Ninehvites turned from their evil ways, Jonah was still angry at God for having compassion on them. He went outside of the city and sat down to see what was going to happen.

Jonah took the step of going to a place of solitude, made himself a little shelter. Then he sat there and stewed. Have you ever done that? I have. Numerous times over the years I would sit by myself and spin all kinds of scenarios of what might happen as I would go through difficult situations. I would dream up all kinds of tales and wish I was a little mouse in the corner just waiting for something to go wrong in the situation so justice would somehow be served. I would stew and spin scenarios. This is not what God intends for our time in solitude!

Jonah was still rebelling against God, even after sitting in the belly of a whale, doing ministry in Ninevah and witnessing a revival. In spite of the rebelling and stewing, God continued to fully provide for Jonah. We see that God even made a vine grow to provide more shade than Jonah could provide for himself. Jonah was angry and chose to continue to be that way. His anger was a form of rebellion that turned to bitterness. Bitterness is a sin needing repentance and it is only through the saving work of the Holy Spirit one can truly overcome this form of rebellion.

During my years of working with the disabled I interacted with many people who remained bitter over their disability even after they were rehabilitated and restored. Granted, many times life had changed forever for these people. But at the same time, it was also evident God had provided for them through their difficult season. Rather than focusing on their healing and restoration, they chose to see only the *what if's and could be's*. Life had not gone as I planned. I had my own times of being in the belly of a whale or times when I sat under a vine provided by God. As I studied Jonah, I began to see my own *what if's and could be's*. At the end of the study, my perception had changed. I no longer saw Jonah as a Bible story figure of a man who survived being swallowed by a fish, but rather a man who sat in solitude after God chose to continue to provide for him. And as Jonah sat in solitude, he chose to make himself miserable by focusing on the wrong things.

God blessed me immeasurably when He could have left me for *dead*. People who wronged me have also been blessed immeasurably. It has been a true exercise of confession and repentance to sit in solitude and put God's compassion into perspective. Even as I am writing, I have this sense I need to continue taking this wanting for God to take revenge and somehow make a wrong right, even when there is very little that is wrong.

Our times of solitude are a waste if we continue to play God, waiting to see what happens next or to watching for the failures of people. Solitude is wasted if we wait for the big event to happen (whatever that might be in your imagination). After participating in the Bible study on Jonah, I thought about how the story of Jonah could have turned out differently, if only Jonah could have gotten over himself. I believe God had this story put into the Scriptures for us as a stark example of what a bitter person looks like. God wants us to see Jonah as an example of a poor outcome when it comes to rebelling in the heart. He wants us to make sure we can rewrite our own stories to overcome the bitterness, better than how Jonah did.

A part of life coaching that is effective is to have the client tell their story. As they tell the story of the past I can help the client to see patterns in their life. They can then make the choice to write a new story. Of course there are roadblocks which may hinder the person in creating a new story, but it is all about taking small steps towards overcoming patterns keeping the client in a rut, repeating the same thing. Bitterness does that to a person. In rewriting the story of Jonah and what he did in his time of solitude as he watched the city of Nineveh restored, I have found I need to sometimes rewrite my own story. What better thing to do as I sit in solitude. What about you?

When you sit in your alone times, what and who do you think about?

Are you at peace or are you stewing, mulling and harboring bitterness?

As you look ahead, what roadblocks may keep you from stepping away from bitterness?

Go to a place of solitude, invite the Holy Spirit to be present and rewrite your life story. Replace the bitterness of the past with compassion and hope. Then visualize what your future story may look like without the bitterness and rebellion in the heart.

On Trying to be God

I am God, a God of compassion and mercy as I demonstrated in times of old. I ask you to turn your heart of bitterness into a vessel of compassion and mercy, even to those who continue to persecute you and taunt you. I know this is a big assignment and I know that it is only with the aid of the Holy Spirit humans can accomplish this. I ask you to spend your times of solitude in writing the story of compassion, love and mercy, even when there are those who do not deserve it. Imagine what a different world it would be if bitterness was replaced by tender mercy. There are always those who are worse off and there are also those who are blessed immeasurably even when they seemingly don't deserve it. But this is not what life is all about. My Word is full of examples where life was not fair. If you search you will see examples of people who rebelled by choosing not to celebrate when goodness over came the bad. Stubborn and rebellious hearts remained in my people even when I brought autumn and spring rains in season (Jeremiah 5:23). It was their choice to make. My sons and daughters, you have a choice too. You can turn the times of solitude into a time of vision. Or you can sit under the vine and stew. In your heart, you know which choice I want you to make. I want you to share in the vision I have for you that you can be a vessel of mercy and compassion. People will see that you have a heart for me. Replace the heart of bitterness and you will discover during your times of solitude my vine of protection and blessing will never dry up and wither away as it did with Jonah.

Bringing Order

*Very early in the morning, while it was still dark, Jesus
got up, left the house and went off to a solitary place,
where he prayed.*
Mark 1:35

There is nothing better to me than the start of a new day in the summer! In the summertime my routine begins by getting up as early as possible, even when I do not have to, so I can enjoy as much day light as possible. I make a pot of coffee, check the bird feeders to see if the raccoons raided them during the night and I sit on my porch to watch the sun rise. In the early summer, the birds are singing and it can be quiet loud. Once they are done mating and have raised their hatches of young ones the mornings are still filled with singing, but it is less intentional and their songs are freer flowing. As the summer wanes and the birds flock together to head south, their songs are more purposeful and there is an air of urgency in them. As I sit with my coffee and watch the hummingbirds at the feeder I marvel at how much energy they have and how they can be so busy with their day already barely before the sun rises.

I will admit I am a morning person and for someone who is not, this scene can be called perhaps disgusting. So I will ask a question. Whatever time of the day you get up, do you take time to put things in order first? From the time Jesus was a young boy and his mother and father found him learning in the temple (Luke 2: 41-50) Jesus was putting things in order regarding his life. Jesus had a habit of disappearing from people. As Mark recorded another one of those times he makes several points. A) very early in the morning, in fact it was before sunrise, b) went away from the house to be by himself, and c) spent time talking to God. What a wonderful way to get organized!

I remember when my children were babies and I would be up with them during the night. Those days were filled with exhaustion and unpredictability. But if I was up with one of them towards morning, sometimes I would stay up and could get a head start on the day's tasks. I would do some laundry, get a meal started ahead of time, and perhaps pay some bills and clean off my desk. This was in my days before I began my journey of walking in a closer relationship with Jesus. Even today if I don't sit down as soon as the coffee is ready, I can go into work mode. Once I am in this mode it is difficult to sit down with my Bible, focus on God and spend time with Him.

If you look at the verses following our passage, you will see Jesus' disciples were the ones who disturbed His time of solitude. The verse has a connotation of urgency in it. It was not just one disciple looking for Jesus either, but rather it could have been most of them. The verse says Simon and his companions were looking for Him. If you have children in the house or do business or work from home, you know what it is like to be interrupted when you just want to be alone. Perhaps that is why Jesus snuck away to His place of solitude when it was still dark.

One of my childhood memories is when I found my mother alone in her bedroom, sitting in her rocking chair. Because living on a farm meant tending to animals and chores early in the morning, her time of solitude was after breakfast when we had gone to school and my dad was outside working. I recently found a poem she wrote about her place of solitude and her time of fellowship with the Lord. I am sure she would not mind me sharing it with you. It is my hope you too will find spending time with the Lord on a regular basis will put life in order for you as it did with my mom. I am learning this for myself.

The Quiet Room
I have a quiet room
In a secret place.
There I meet my secret love.
Together we hold such sweet communion
That the entire room seems filled
With love.
And joy and peace.

My house was empty once.
A total void.
Then He came in.

I met Him and talked to Him
And He to me
In my house and in His house.
But a room remained closed.
No joy or peace.
I cried out in desperation
For joy and peace.
And love.
Then He sent a Helper
To bring to my remembrance
All that He had said.
And suddenly the door to that room
Burst open
The room was filled with light.
And I beheld my Love
As though for the first time.
And joy
And peace.

So I go to that room
At any moment
For rest and refreshment.
And often the room is so filled
With the sweetness of that love.
That the joy and peace of it
Overflows
And fills the entire house.
And life is beautiful
Because it's filled
With Love.

M.A.B.

As you look at your life, habits and patterns, when do you find the best time to slip away into the secret place of solitude where you can put life in order?

When you are alone during that time, do your thoughts race and bounce around?

Do you focus on self, can you quiet your spirit, can you focus on the One who brings order to life?

As you spend regular time alone, ask the Holy Spirit to come into your presence, open your Bible, perhaps to a favorite chapter or verse or just allow him to fill your heart as He did in my Mom's secret place. What is He saying to you?

The Secret Place

My son, Jesus knew where to find me. As he slipped away from His disciples in the early morning before dawn He came to have fellowship with me. We talked and He put His earthly life in order. He prayed, but it was not one sided. We conversed and He was able to make sense of the human side of His being. As you spend time with me in solitude to bring things of life into order, this is what I want of you, my friend. I want you to be with me regularly, to find peace and joy and love in the secret rooms of your heart. I know there are rooms in your heart that need a helper. This is why I sent my Holy Spirit. It is only through the help of my Spirit you can find the peace that will bring true order to life. With peace in your heart, you will know what righteousness is. With this you will be able to speak truth from the heart (Psalm 15:2). With the world in chaos, truth needs to be spoken. As Jesus put His life in order so He could speak truth to a chaotic world, so the same is for you today. Come to the place of solitude. Ask the Holy Spirit to come into the secret rooms of your heart. When the secret rooms of your heart are put in order with Truth, your life will be put in order. Be ready to be filled with joy and love and peace. For it is only then there will be order to life. Go away to a solitary place to put life in order. I am waiting to meet you there.

Provision and Protection

*By day the Lord went ahead of them in a pillar of cloud
to guide them on their way and by night in a pillar of
fire to give them light. So they could travel by day or
night. Neither the pillar of cloud by day nor the pillar of
fire by night left its place in front of the people.*
Exodus 13:21-22

Spending time in solitude is a good thing. But it can also be a time of trial and testing, a true desert experience. Hardly a person on this earth gets through life without a desert experience and for many of us we experience this more than once. Most often it is after a loss, perhaps a home, divorce or death. Loss of job, dreams, purpose and vision can also bring a desert time.

A lesson that was hard for me to grasp, learn *and* believe was the fact that God would provide and protect me no matter what part of the desert I was in. The scar of unbelief and distrust came from my view point of connecting my earthly father and heavenly Father as having the same characteristics. Once I established the fact in my mind that my heavenly Father is not a sinful human, my perspective began to change. This meant that heavenly Father would never fail me. Even after everything God brought me through and gave me, every promise of healing, restoration, provision and protection, I still had doubt. When I looked at life through my own unhealed eyes, I had difficulty believing he would always be there for me.

The solitude of the wilderness experience is truly a time when God gives us the opportunity to witness His cloud of protection and pillar of fire for provision. During a part of my wilderness time I did several little exercises to test and also remember my God as one of protection and provision. The first test I did was for thirty days; I wrote down one thing God surprised me with each day. Sometimes at the end of the day

I would have to think for a minute, but not once did God not show up in some way.

The second thing I did was I made a list of the trials during the wilderness time. Some time later I would go back and look at that list again. In revisiting the trials I would marvel that it had not been as bad as it seemed at the time. It was because God brought me through with a *cloud by day and pillar of fire by night.* One such wilderness time of solitude was after I broke my wrist. I had the worst pain I ever experienced. Not only that, but I had no disability insurance, my vacation time had been used up, medical bills were mounting from the two surgeries required to repair the fracture and I was living alone.

It was during this time I (as best as I could since my writing hand was in a cast) when I made a list of how God was giving protection and provision for me. Protection came in that we had several snowstorms and I did not need to drive in them since I was not able to work at the time. It came through bill collectors having grace and not threatening me. It came through having a wise orthopedist who knew how much I could work once the cast came off. Provision came through financial help from my church, the son of a friend who shoveled my driveway and walks, my German Shepherd, Lilly, who laid alongside the couch day after day, providing companionship, friends who took me to doctor appointments or run errands for me and my prayer partners who were faithful to me. This wilderness time of solitude was different than other wilderness times I experienced previously. It was easier for me to track how God was working and the experience did not leave me scarred except for the one on my wrist, the result of the surgeries.

Other wilderness times were more difficult and much longer than a just a few months. But during those times the provision and protection were greater and deeper. In looking at the wilderness time of the Israelites, God gave them the cloud and fire right after they crossed the Red Sea. However, Pharaoh and his army had not been destroyed yet (Exodus 13). In fact they were in hot pursuit and the Israelites were hemmed in with no place to flee. But God, as only God can do, parted the Red Sea and let them get pretty close! Then He used far more than a cloud or fire to protect and provide for His people. He used a miracle saving work to deliver them once and for all from the Egyptian oppression.

Do we see the cloud of protection and pillar of fire of provision on a day to day basis but miss the bigger miracles or opportunities of deliverance resulting from solitude in the wilderness? I think this is more of where I need to focus. God provided the miracles of deliverance in my life, time and time again. I was delivered from an abusive marriage. I was delivered from bad and unhealthy jobs. I was delivered from heartbreaking relationships. And I was delivered from the pain and destruction of my past. Oh, the obstacles that became opportunities!

This is how big God is. He is a God of hope and it is only through Him we will see the big miracles of deliverance. No one ever expected our big God to deliver us from our sins through His son Jesus dying on the cross and rising again. The prophets talked of it and there were people who believed it ahead of time, but when it was actually happening, most were oblivious to the fact God was in action. My wilderness times were much the same way. During the ordeal, I did not always see God at work. In fact, most of the time I cried out "God, where are you?" Even as I sit here writing today, reflecting on the parts of my life that are remnants of the wilderness, I think to my self, "Have you let me down, God?" But more likely it is this: God has His cloud of provision and pillar of fire of protection in front of me and somewhere in the future there will be a big miracle of deliverance!

If you are in a wilderness time in life, what evidence is there of clouds of provision and pillars of fire of protection from God?

Have you seen a miracle of deliverance from any of your wilderness experiences?

What keeps you in the place of not believing God will continue being your provider and protector?

What step or action can you take to align your thinking with the truth God will always protect and provide for you?

My Protection, Provision and Deliverance

I loved my people, the Israelites. You too, are mine and I love you just the same. Out of that love I am your protector and provider and when necessary, your deliverer. During your wilderness time, is there anything you lack? If you do, is it out of desire or necessity? If you need protection is it from someone or something or from yourself? I am available for all of this. In this time of solitude in the wilderness, there is much to be learned. Learn to lean on me, trust me, believe me and have hope in me. Do not look ahead, but only to the cloud and the fire right in front of you. That is all you need for this time. Trust that if you need a miracle of deliverance, I will do that too. It won't be too late, although you may question my timing. I am a God of surprises and I ask you track that. Some days the surprises will be obvious and other days they will not be as obvious to the human eye. You may be surprised by my faithfulness. Even when there is no answer to the trial in the time of wilderness solitude, my faithfulness will prevail. When my timing is right and the miracle of deliverance needs to happen, I will be there (Psalm 78). I work in ways unknown to man as you can see time and time again in Scripture. Many people have endured the solitude of the wilderness time, just as the Israelites did. Keep the pillar cloud of protection in front of you to give you direction. Keep the pillar of fire of provision in front of you to give you light. I will be there. This is my promise. Believe me and love me and I will do the rest.

A Time of Testing

*Jesus, full of the Holy Spirit, returned from the Jordon
and was led by the Spirit into the desert, where for forty
days he was tempted by the devil.*
Luke 4:1

One of the most profound examples of being in a time and state of solitude is in the story of Jesus spending forty days alone in the desert alone with the devil! Jesus had three altercations with Satan during this time. And of course, being without sin, perfect in every way and without a hint of blemish, He was able to withstand the tests even though the devil was hard at work. I have often thought about how the course of events would have changed had Jesus not been able to withstand those temptations. This is a pivotal time in the Gospels. The story of salvation could have ended here and anything else that would have happened after would have been pointless. At this point the good news of salvation would have bottomed out like Adam and Eve did in the Garden of Eden. Either a new story or a new savior would have had to emerge or there would be not salvation or eternal life for us! So this time in the desert was huge in shaping the course of events, not only for Jesus, but for all mankind, including you and me.

As a life coach my role is not to dissect, analyze and counsel clients about their past. If they have unresolved issues requiring counseling and healing from the past a better route is to see a counselor. However, in life coaching we use events of the past to help the client see how God can now use those times to take steps forward in a positive and God pleasing way for the future. Almost always for my client there is a true desert time when the client faced choices, reality, and the consequences of those choices. When the client understands that the test and temptation they failed is part of their story, they can then take the step to allow God to use it for His purpose and glory.

One of my own desert times of solitude was when I was in college. I was fresh off the farm and going to school in the inner city. I was alone a lot and the sole purpose was to get done with school so I could launch my career. I did well with choices during this time, only because of the covering of prayer from my parents, God's protective hand over me and my single focus on the future. During other times when I was in the desert I didn't fare as well. Emotionally drained from surviving an abusive marriage I was faced with the temptation of having an affair. Details are not important, except that I was vulnerable and weak and the devil knew it. I was in a desert time of solitude. I remember well the moment when the temptation began. It was before I had a thought about having the affair, much less with the person I did. One day I was standing in the mirror getting ready to go somewhere. I told myself, "My husband doesn't love me, but maybe someday I will find someone who does." This was the moment when the devil was there and the course of events in my life was changed forever. Are you rationalizing to yourself as I did for just a short time after "Who wouldn't have thought this, if the marriage was abusive?" Or perhaps you are minimizing the thought which eventually led to an event by saying "It happens all the time."

It took years after the affair and only through the saving and healing work of the Holy Spirit I was able to move beyond the guilt and shame. My thoughts were that because I had committed a *big sin,* I was not worthy of God's love and grace any more. Looking back I now see how God placed people and circumstances in my life to provide healing and restoration. Today, as a result of the good and the bad, my driving passion is to encourage others to be healed and restored. I want others to experience the restoration God desires for each of, regardless of how big or little, the un-resisted temptations leading to sin were.

Jesus was tempted three times by the devil. He was tempted to turn a stone into bread. He had not eaten in days and the devil knew he was hungry. So Jesus was tempted physically. Then the devil tempted him spiritually by telling him if he bowed to him the world would be His, in other words, the eventual suffering on the cross would not be His. And finally the devil tempted Jesus emotionally by giving Jesus the idea to create drama. What a scene it would have been if Jesus had thrown Himself from the highest point of the temple.

If you look closely at this story there is one singular thing making this story possible for Jesus to withstand these three temptations. The one singular aspect is in the first phrase of the theme verse, *Jesus, full of the Holy Spirit*. If Jesus didn't have help of the Holy Spirit in the solitude of the wilderness, how would have things gone? Would he have been able to do it alone, even in his divine nature? We will never know. God's sovereignty was above the devil and He made sure the course of events happened as they did. If you look at the chapter just before the temptation, Jesus was baptized and the Spirit descended on him. God, in His divine wisdom made sure Jesus was prepared to withstand the solitude time of being alone with the devil.

I can't go back and change the course of my life anymore than you can. The horrible times of solitude, of being one on one with the devil looks a little different for everyone. For someone who struggles with addiction, it is in sneaking a drink, a cigarette, a look at a nude photo, or taking a hit or going to a casino. For someone who struggles with power and control it can be taking advantage of an opportunity to act on the need for control, thus hurting whoever is in that realm of power. For others it can be the temptation when alone, to compensate by shopping, excessive eating, and ungodly sexual activity. Temptation includes perseverating on and scheming to get even with others. All are physical, emotional and spiritual temptations.

This is the three fold triune God coming up against the temptations from the devil. Jesus withstood the horrible solitude with the devil. And we can too. It begins by asking Him to help and He will. But remember: it is only with the help of the *Holy Spirit* and the sovereignty, love and grace of our heavenly father that anyone can withstand and overcome the temptations of the devil.

What events and temptations in solitude have you encountered?

How have they shaped your present?

How do you anticipate those times of solitude with the devil in shaping your future?

Have you ever intentionally asked the Holy Spirit to enter into your life? This may be the pivotal time that shapes your future as the desired way God intends for you.

Temptation and Love

My dearest one, I saw my son Jesus being tempted in every way possible. He experienced every aspect of humanness to prove He was indeed an earthly man. I knew it would be difficult and that is why I provided an outpouring of the Holy Spirit to come to His aid. Jesus did not fall. Solitude can be an invitation for the devil. It can be during a time when you are vulnerable or it can be when you think you are above temptation and sin. Even the human kin of Jesus succumbed to the temptation of the devil when King David was tempted and failed the test (2 Samuel 11). You are not alone in your solitude and temptation with the devil. I am sending the Holy Spirit to your aid. All you need to do is invite Him to help. Invite Him to come and pour Himself into the very core of your being, your heart. Let Him come pouring into your mind, will and emotions. There will be temptations in the future, but regardless, you are mine and I love you more than you know. I want you to learn to withstand those times with the help of my Spirit. David cried out after he failed in being tempted, "Wash me and I will be whiter than snow. Create in me a pure heart, O God, and renew a steadfast spirit within me. Restore to me the joy of your salvation" (Psalm 51:7, 10, and 12). As you cry out too, and seek help, know I am hearing your cry. Don't try to resist temptation alone. Jesus had help. Will you also seek that same help?

Final Thoughts on Solitude

Solitude can be a time in a person's life, an event or the result of a situation. It can be for a season or for just a brief time during the day. It can be self imposed or the result of consequences or because of God's sovereignty. From your time of solitude I would like you to remember these things.

In solitude you can:

1) find direction from God
2) find peace that comes only from God
3) find the ability to endure
4) find refuge from the world
5) gain perspective
6) experience God's sovereignty
7) spend time unwashed
8) encounter God
9) find clarity
10) stop rebelling
11) bring order to life
12) find protection and provision
13) overcome temptation

SILENCE

Silence

Silence can be the result of solitude and ties in with simplicity. To find silence you may need to be alone in solitude. You may need to go to a place of simplicity to find silence. Silence can be awkward and unsettling. Silence may leave you asking "Is there anyone out there?" When someone you love is silent it may lead you to wonder, opening the door to fear or other unwanted emotions.

During this time in silence, you may find it hard to find. You may find your fears come glaring out at you. Or you may experience a time of silence as a haven, a time of just *being*. As you study the Scripture verses in this section it is my hope you will discover how silence can take you another step forward in your relationship with God.

I discovered during my wilderness time that at times silence was my friend and at other times my enemy. I found I have a choice as to what to do with silence. Yet even today, I can make silence a good thing or I let it work against what God has in store for me. As you journey through this section on silence, learn from silence, embrace it and love it. I hope you are looking forward to what God has in store for you.

Silence in the Heart

Peace I leave with you, my peace I give you, not as the
world gives do I give you. Let not your heart troubled,
neither let it be afraid.
John 14:27

This Bible verse was imprinted on my heart at the tender age of fourteen. It is my confirmation verse. The old white haired pastor who picked this verse for me must have prayed about which verse from thousands of other Bible verses. This is the verse God wanted me to have for my own. Confirmation in my church was a time for young people to affirm their faith in God. The year prior to this affirmation was spent on structured study of the doctrines of our church. It called for a lot of memorizing and most of what I recollect from my fourteen year-old view point is it was that memorization was tedious and boring. Sounds like a typical fourteen year-old, doesn't it?

The culmination of this year of intensive study was on a Sunday in early April. The thing I remember most clearly about this particular Sunday was how muddy our farm was! It must have been a rough Minnesota winter followed by a lot of rain. I don't remember much about the church service which is when we received our confirmation verses, nor do I remember much about the rigorous questioning in regards to the doctrines and creeds my church denomination upheld. We answered those questions in front of the entire congregation. This event for our class was meant to be an affirmation of our faith in Jesus Christ as our Savior and it is only through his suffering on the cross and rising again that we would go to heaven. But for me it was a day of nervousness and extreme self-consciousness. My time of true acceptance of Jesus as my Savior and wanting to be in relationship with him would come several years later. At the end of Confirmation Day, the John 14:27 verse was tucked away with all the other memorabilia of the event, not to be looked at again until twenty years later. In hindsight I wish the emphasis of my confirmation day had been on our chosen Bible verses, rather than the rituals of the day. How it could have been a source of help and comfort sooner than twenty years later.

Fast forward twenty years. Life was fast paced. There was never silence in the house. I had two little very busy boys, a business with the office in the home and a marriage tattered and frayed from years of abuse. There was almost never a time of silence. Not only was there never silence, but my heart was troubled. I struggled with anxiety and fear. I needed help and did not know where to go. I was wrapped up in putting on a good front. I was hurting and I had no idea what the future held. Later in my speaking and consulting on family violence I described it as looking into a *black hole*. From my worldly standpoint and limited vision, I could not see a sign of hope for my future. The cycle of abuse continued to escalate. The anxiety continued to mount and my heart was more and more troubled. I prayed God would silence my heart. I gravitated between heart pounding fear and the depression of hopelessness.

Just before I put an end to the cycle of fear, anxiety, craziness and trouble in our home, I found my confirmation verse. There it was, John 4:27. It was a direct message from Jesus. Do not be afraid. Do not let your heart be troubled. I could silence it with a peace the *world* does not give. From then on it did not matter what my future held. I did not look ahead or worry about the future. Jesus had given me the promise that I could have peace in my heart and at that particular moment I knew Jesus was speaking to *me!* I clung to that promise and I did not have to struggle with anxiety over my present circumstances or my future any longer. From then on there was a calmness and silence in my heart I had never known. It was a peace that is almost indescribable and the fears, anxiety and depression that had been screaming and gnawing away in my mind and heart were silenced.

Silence and peace can be synonymous. What links the two together is Jesus. Only He can replace all the hard stuff the world throws at us. Whatever happens to us while we live here on this earth can be replaced by knowing Jesus. To know Him and be in relationship with Him is the only way to once and for all put all the hurts and hardships in the heart to silence. I wish I hadn't lived for twenty years without fully understanding and experiencing my confirmation verse. Thankfully I found it again when I did. In the nearly twenty years since I found John 14:27 it has been a source of hope and comfort on many a day when my heart needs to be silenced and at peace. Jesus is the only true antidote for anxiety.

For years I struggled, trying to have the peace in my heart it desperately desired and needed. I knew from my upbringing as a believer in Christ that a personal relationship with Jesus was the answer, but the tricky part came in trying to connect the mind and the heart. What I knew in my mind and what I wanted in my heart were two different things. Through the *deep waters* of breaking the cycle of abuse in my family I learned firsthand how Jesus gives peace to the troubled heart. Through this knowledge and God's demonstration of it He would be present through each minute detail of the ordeal, I witnessed how He would resolve each anxious thought I had about my life.

In the time since, my journey of dealing with anxiety has been like a roller coaster ride. Some days I do better with managing it than others. It depends on my state of mind, my perception, and if I am walking the daily walk with Jesus. When I do, the anxiety, on a scale of 0 out of 10, is a "0". When I try to manage anxiety from the worldly point of view or on my own, it hovers around 7/10, unless it is a bad day and then it escalates to 10/10—out of control! Applying the principle of this Bible verse is a daily walk. The enemy knows the best way to paralyze me is to implant anxious thoughts in my head. When this happens, my heart disconnects and anxiety spins out of control. The keys for me in managing anxiety are to remember how God brought me through circumstances I never imagined would happen. The second key is for me to remember to live intentionally in a relationship with Jesus.

What is your heart saying to you?

Is your in a state of fear, anxiety, troubled, depression and hopelessness?

What is your mind telling you?

Jayne Kane

What have you tried to do to calm the troubled heart as *the world* would have you try?

What is Jesus saying to you that will silence the turmoil and put your heart at peace?

The Troubled Heart

Do not be afraid my troubled child. I am here with you to give you peace. It is a peace that surpasses all understanding and will silence even the most troubled heart. The peace I give is not the temporary peace people grasp for as they meander through the troubles of living in this deprived and temporary world. The peace I give comes from the love of my son, Jesus. It is only through what He did on the cross and then when He rose again that brings real peace. The troubled heart is plagued with fear and worry. Anxiety and depression sets in and rather than silence and peace in the heart, a battle rages. Focus on Jesus. Let His love permeate your troubled heart. As the pounding of the heart is silenced, let your heart rest in His love. As you whisper His name, listen to the silence that follows. As you focus on the love of Jesus, know there is no need for anxiety. As you rest and are silenced, feel the beat of your heart, notice your soul is no longer anxious. As you breathe and feel the anxiety leave, rest assured it is because you are replacing it with the love of Jesus, the almighty power of God Himself and the work of the Holy Spirit. Leave your troubles, rest and let your heart be silenced. The peace I give you which goes beyond human understanding will guard you heart and mind through my son, Jesus (Philippians 4:7).

A Time to be Silent

There is a time for everything, and a season for every activity under heaven: a time to be silent and a time to speak.
Ecclesiastes 3:1, 7

I recently received a call from a family member who wanted my opinion on something. I didn't want to express my thoughts because I did not want to offend anyone. I was taken off guard by the call and did not have time to form a kind, but honest opinion to offer. So I stayed silent, for what seemed like a long minute. I was struggling to find the right words without creating hurt, but at the same time I was asked to give my honest opinion. In the end my silence became the target of the conflict. My silence was interpreted as creating awkwardness and as being rude. It was the last thing I wanted to happen and I was simply trying to be nice. But it got me thinking about silence. When is silence good and when is it not? There are people who are never silent and there are others who rarely speak. When a person of few words speaks, people tend to lean a little closer and pay close attention. At the same time, some people just never shut up; we know the type.

There was a scar in my past I had to deal with during my time of healing and restoration. This scar was the result of my own interpretation of silence from people. There was a time when I had a false perception of silence and it was when I didn't hear from a friend for a while I questioned if I said or did something to offend this person. When I was going through my divorce I interpreted the silence of my friends as taking the other side. And even today, an extended time of not having contact with friends leaves me feeling isolated. Of course the antidote to this is to pick up the phone and call someone.

During my divorce, the silence of my church was almost a bigger struggle than the circumstances surrounding the divorce itself. Once again, my interpretation was that my church did not care or did not want to stand up for what was godly. The truth was, no one felt empowered to speak up. Years later, several church members came to me apologizing for not speaking up and not taking a stand on how the church should have dealt with the divorce. So a scar was left that needed to be healed. Just as my phone conversation had an awkward silence, there can be other times of awkward silence. In life coaching one of the skills we develop is the art of embracing silence. When a client is processing or thinking about a question it is the life coaches' responsibility to allow and foster silence for processing. It is a beneficial aspect of life coaching and many times silence is followed by an *aha* moment. And yet there are people who find any time of silence to be uncomfortable.

I have noticed there are some people who can't be alone or when they are alone they must have a radio or television on. Why is this? How does that person perceive silence? Through the years I learned the hard lesson of being silent, even when I do not feel like it or when I have a strong opinion on something. The need to speak up is a way of being in control. Most of the time when a person is trying to be in control, the action following is usually counterproductive and even destructive.

The blessings of living in the upper Midwest are the four distinct seasons. It has been said there is a season for everyone and everything. This is what Ecclesiastes 3 is also saying. In reading the whole passage of Ecclesiastes 3 it lists a number of activities and a season for each of them.

My favorite season is spring, just as it was as when I was a little girl wandering the pasture and wading in the pond our farm. Nearly everyone in our region has a favorite season and a reason why it is a favorite. Seasons come and seasons go. In the Midwest, spring can be short and cool. The summers can also be short and there are years when it seems as though we skip spring and go right from winter to summer. An overwhelming favorite season of Minnesotans is autumn. Most years the autumn season is crisp, colorful and refreshing. Then there are those who embrace and even love the winter and all it has to offer. One sure thing is that the seasons will come and go.

This concept and truth is because of one thing: God's sovereignty. The changing seasons are one of God's most dramatic demonstrations of God's control. Of course there is scientific rationale of what happens when the seasons change and it is fascinating and very complex. But is still comes down to the fact that all this happens because of God's timing and His love for us and creation, even when He sees so much going wrong.

A reality of life is that we as humans have very little control over life and no control over changes and the seasons we experience. It comes down to the fact that the God we know is sovereign and He is in control, whether we want Him to be or not. Yes, it is true that He has given humans a free will, the ability to make choices and decisions. But when it comes right down to it, even in spite of our blunderings of having a free will, God will always have His way.

To overcome my need to have control of my life and to be silent more often, I find myself frequently asking God to give me wisdom. I need wisdom for when to speak and when to be silent. I also need wisdom as to when to act and when to do nothing. And I need wisdom to make the godly choice rather than doing it my own impulsive way. Recently I asked God to give me wisdom and discernment for the season He has me in, including when to be silent and when to speak up. There is another passage in Ecclesiastes that speaks to this. It is found in chapter 9 verses 17 and 18, "The quiet words of the wise are more to be heeded than the shouts of a ruler of fools. Wisdom is better than weapons of war, but one sinner destroys much good."

I would rather have God be in charge of the seasons of creation and show His marvelous display of sovereignty and have Him in charge of the seasons of my life than me be in charge. This includes being in a season of silence. There are times to be silent and when to speak. The only way to truly have God be in control is to operate under His divine control and allow Him to show me when the time is right. But it means being silent long enough to let Him speak those words of wisdom to me.

What is a season of silence like to you?

What circumstances have you found yourself in where you wanted to speak up but knew it would destroy the potential good?

Do you believe that God is sovereign and in control or do you find yourself taking control rather than being silent?

How do you perceive silence from others?

What part of silence do you need to give to the sovereign control of God?

Is it the silence of others, the person who never shuts up, is it your own need to be in control through speaking? Or is it desire for wisdom for the season you are in?

The Seasons

I am in control of the universe, the creation and the seasons. I am also in control of humanity, even though many do not believe this. I am your sovereign God and ultimately I have dominion over all of this. Just as there are the seasons of creation, so there are the seasons to act. The challenge for you, my people, is to have the wisdom to know what season it is. Is it a time to speak or a time to be silent? Is it a time to have quiet words, rather than shouting like a fool? I know the struggle you are in. I know the enemy tells you to take control and break the silence. I know that he says you can be in charge and be sovereign too. The seasons of creation are beautiful in every way and they are constantly changing, just as life on this earth is always changing. I know that for many people there is so much that is changing and always unpredictable it is hard to believe there is anyone in control. These are the times when an extra measure of wisdom is needed. Discernment of the season is crucial. These are the times when you need to give me complete control. My Spirit will advise you about speaking and being silent. But for the Spirit to speak, you need to be silent. The winter season can be harsh, the summer season stifling, the autumn season may lack luster and the spring season can be muddy. But I am in my temple, all the earth be silent (Habakkuk 2:20). Trust me, I am sovereign and just as one season fades to another, there will be another season for you too.

The Stillness

Be still and know that I am God.
Psalm 46:10

This Bible verse is so simple, yet so profound. I have a painting in my living room of a loon sitting among the lily pads and cattails. The water is perfectly still, smooth and glassy in this picture. *Be still and know I am God* is inscribed in the frame and anyone who looks at this painting can easily imagine the loon sitting there perfectly still and silent.

This painting is a wonderful reminder of my times of camping. I loved sitting in a boat on the lake in the early morning with the fog rising from it, the golden sunrise making its way up from the horizon and the majestic pines standing as a back drop, perfectly silent, not even a whisper coming from them. I would sit and listen to the silence and wonder how long it would be before someone or something would break it. Most often it was a loon or a fisherman's boat motor breaking the perfect silence. Up to that point it was as though all of creation was worshipping God in perfect silence.

The painting in my living room has a calming affect and is a wonderful visual image of the marvel of God's creation in *still motion*. God knows I have a tough time of sitting still in silence, letting God be God. He also knows that in my lifetime there were times where the waters of life were not smooth or glassy, but instead were rough and choppy and sometimes even over the top of the boat. If you have ever been in a boat where the water is so rough it is coming over the top and is at risk of capsizing, you know the best thing to do is to sit still. Rocking the boat at this point will not help. In fact it may even cause the boat to capsize. Not only have I experienced the glassy silence of the lake, but I have also experienced being in a boat when the lake was rough and windy. My emotions and thoughts were of awe. "We have a big God, because He is even bigger than this storm." I am thinking the psalmist who wrote Psalm 46 must have experienced God's power at some point too. Looking at the whole chapter the writer acknowledges that God is our refuge and strength and an ever present help in trouble. He then goes on to describe events such as earthquakes causing mountains to fall and waters to roar. God's power is not something to be reckoned with!

There is something about God's command to be still that strikes me. He is very direct, to the point and is not requesting us to be still, but instead is exercising His authority and is commanding us to be still and *know* He is God. The catchy phrase I have seen could be the paraphrase for this verse: *Let God be God.* So we are to be still and silent and know God is in control and is all powerful. That is easier said than done, especially when is seems as though God is being silent too. My own mind tends to run like this *"Well, if God is silent on this subject or problem or situation or whatever may be going on, I may as well do something about it myself."* Or other times I will think "Maybe God wants to use me to help Him and if He doesn't, He will stop me." Unfortunately, all too often I am already in the middle of making a mess by the time something or someone stops me.

One of the most dangerous things I can do is to try to be God. Of course He wants me to be godly in my day to day life, but He doesn't want me to take over His role as being the God of the universe. By trying to be God, most often I find it is more so what I say than what I do to *play God.* Just a few minutes ago, my grown son was telling me about a situation where he had an opinion and made a decision based on this. I did not necessarily agree with it and if I had not been writing on the subject of silence, I would have perhaps tried to interject my opinion. Then he would have gotten frustrated with me and I would have gotten in the way of God helping my son with his decision making process. So I stayed silent and just listened. My son did not want my opinion, help or anything else. He just wanted to vent and have somebody to talk to. So under my breath I told myself, "Be still and I am going to let you be God, God!" I can pat myself on the back this time for being silent, even though it was really hard. Because it is not my nature to be silent, the next time I am in that position, I may not do as well.

By being still and silent during critical times in life, such as when the *boat is rocking,* we acknowledge God as powerful enough to handle things on His own. Being still and silent then becomes an act of worship to God. If you look closely at Psalm 46 again you will see that it is a Psalm of praise for God's majesty, deliverance and how He blesses His people.

During a time with the Lord sometime ago I was given a visual image of my life that brought me back to Psalm 46:10. I was sitting alone in a little green wooden boat on a lake. The water around it was lapping up against the sides of it, but was not coming over the top. The water out beyond the boat was perfectly still and glassy. There I was in the little green boat, hanging on for dear life, sitting perfectly still and silent. I know God was showing me that if I hang onto Him for dear life (just as I did in the little green boat) when the rough times in life try to take over, He will take me to the still waters. As I sat in the little boat alone in silence, there was not a thing I could do to get to the still waters by myself. It was all up to the boat. In life, if we sit still and silent and allow God to take charge He will take us to still waters.

When the waters of life are raging around you, do you try to take control and be God, or do you *let God be God?*

What happens during those times when you try to be God?

What happens when you are still and silent?

What situations in life take you to the brink of taking control yourself rather than allowing God to be in control?

What step can you take to worship God through being still and silent as hard as it may be at times?

My Power

 Allow me to be God. I am commanding you to be still and silent and let me do what I will do. I am all knowing and all powerful and I do not need your help to accomplish what I want to do. I know at times it seems as though I am the silent one. In actuality, I am at work and it is only your perception that I am being silent and still. There are times I want you to act on my behalf, but mostly I want you to worship me by acknowledging my power. It is a dangerous thing when humans play God and it grieves me. Silence is a blessing and being still is a discipline. If you are questioning your reason for not wanting to being still and silent, check the motives of your heart (1 Corinthians 4:5). Check what you are telling yourself about the situation and what you are telling yourself about me. Power when not directed by me is a dangerous thing and it can be destructive. The waters of life are navigated best when I am left to be in control. Only I have the ability to still the rough waters on the lakes and seas, and ultimately only I have the power to still the rough waters of life. Cling to me as you would if you were in a boat. Be still and the rough waves of life will be silenced. My child, be still and remember I am God. As I command you to be still, I am also commanding you to <u>know</u> that I am God. By knowing, I am commanding you to experience my power. As you sit still and be silent, experience it and see how I am Lord of the creation, including your life.

Resting in Quietness

In repentance and rest is your salvation; in quietness and
trust is your strength, but you would have none of it.
Isaiah 30:15

One of my favorite childhood memories was how we spent our Sundays. The day began with going to church. Then we would have a dinner that was more representatives of what brunch is. After we were done eating my dad always took a nap. Sometimes my grandparents would come and visit or we would visit them. Occasionally we would go for a drive to bird watch or spend time in nature. Of course, chores had to be done both morning and night as the animals needed to be fed and taken care of. The field work or other heavy chores were saved for the next day although my dad was not strict about what got done on Sunday. In fact, if the hay was dry, ready to be baled and rain was in the forecast he would go to the field and bale whatever was ready. He tried to be practical, but still reserved Sunday as a quiet day, the Sabbath day.

I remember a time in my life when life was the opposite. It just sort of happened. Little by little I was doing more and more on Sunday. The day still started with church, but then errands, chores and the to-do list that did not get done during the week were squeezed in. This type of hectic Sunday resulted from trying to maintain control of life. Eventually I added things I wanted to work on to get a head start on the week. My rationale was if I started the week ahead, then by the end of the week I wouldn't be behind. And maybe, just maybe next Sunday I would be able rest and have a quiet day. But the cycle continued. Every week Sunday was the catch-up day and gradually I began to burn out on life. Does this sound familiar? What had happened since the time when my parents set the example of what the silence and quiet of the Sabbath was truly all about? Being quiet, still, silent and observing the Sabbath has become counter cultural. Gradually, the temptations, stresses and burdens of living in our society have overtaken the silence and quiet of the Sabbath.

There was a pivotal event that changed my view of the Sabbath and empowered me to begin honoring the Sabbath again, as I did as a child. It began when my family was scattered to the winds. My boys went off to college, my husband was gone, and suddenly Sundays weren't the same. They were silent and void and it no longer mattered if I worked all day or left the chores, errands and cares for the week ahead. Sundays became a day of silence. During one of my college classes on discipleship, my perception and attitude towards the Sabbath was changed forever. I was humbled by the fact that I had subtly slipped into the trap of thinking I did not need a Sabbath.

As I coach my clients, I see those who are in the trap of *go, go, go, crash and burn* cycle. They may or may not recuperate and repeat the same cycle again. As Isaiah was talking to the rebellious Israelites, they must have been in the same type of cycle, not allowing a time for quiet, rest, silence and Sabbath. As Isaiah refers to quietness, rest, strength and trust he finishes the verse by saying, "You would have none of it."

There are two other key words in this verse that cannot be ignored. Isaiah says that in repentance and rest there is salvation. If you look closely at this verse Isaiah is giving the formula for restoration of the soul. The formula is this:

* To be restored in body, mind, and spirit you need to have a time of repentance and rest. To find strength you need to have a time of quietness and trust. Salvation can only be fully understood when you experience these things. This is what the Sabbath is for.

God rested after He was done with creation. Why should mere humans think they are above needing a designated time of rest? Quiet, silence, repentance, rest, trust, salvation sounds like a Sabbath day to me. It is what the Sabbath day or the Sundays of my childhood were made up of. It is interesting that the root word of restoration is rest. It takes rest to be restored. It takes being quiet and silent and sometimes being alone to be restored. As hard as we try to take shortcuts to be restored there are none. Being quiet and silent is a way to allow the Holy Spirit to do the work of bringing repentance to a person's heart and soul.

Obviously, observing the Sabbath on Sunday cannot be honored by everyone. There have been times in my career when I was assigned to work on Sunday and this is the case for many people. But what God is asking for and modeled at the beginning of creation is to take a day once a week and set it aside as a Sabbath day, a day for silence and quiet, for spiritual reflection, renewal and for restoration. Silence is the hidden key in all of this. It is essential if a person wants to be fully restored. It is in silence a person can hear the voice of God and can know tomorrow will bring a new day. But for today He wants us to focus on restoration.

What are your habits on your Sabbath Day or don't you have a Sabbath Day?

What are you things you tell yourself on the Sabbath Day?

If you could change one thing to honor the Sabbath Day, as outlined in the formula, what would it be?

What do you need to do to be restored physically, emotionally and spiritually, not just a part of you, but in all three parts?

My Day for You

 I have a gift for you, my people. It is a day of rest. I frequently gave examples of the Sabbath in Scripture. I made it part of the laws of life as written in the Ten Commandments (Leviticus 22:3). I modeled it when I finished creation (Genesis 2:2). Why do you not want to take this as a gift of restoration? What keeps you from wanting to have a day of rest and to be silenced in the heart and soul? The rebellious Israelites would have none of it. They did not understand the need for silence or quietness. They were an obstinate nation and went against the very grain of how I created them. Please do not do the same. I know there are those who feel guilty for taking time to be restored. But even the fields of the earth need a time of rest after the harvest (Leviticus 25:5). It is how I ordained it from the very beginning. As my co-worker on this earth I want to give you the gift of a time not only for a weekly Sabbath of silence and quiet, but also a time where each day you take time for silence and rest. True restoration of the body, mind and spirit only happens when that time is taken. So rest, be silent and be quiet. Take a day for reflection, rest and restoration of the soul (Jeremiah 6:16). Be renewed and strengthened. Reflect on your salvation through my saving work in Jesus and you will be refreshed.

Silence to Bring Balance

He makes me lie down in green pastures, he leads me
beside quiet waters, he restores my soul.
Psalm 23:2-3

One of the challenges I face as a gardener is to find ways to bring balance to my gardens. When I design one, it is usually with a theme that will hopefully bring uniformity, interest and character to the garden. My biggest and oldest garden is the old fashioned perennial garden. Many of the plants in this flower garden are perennials I dug on my parent's farm over twenty years ago. They include peonies, black eyed Susan, garden phlox, babies' breath, balloon flowers and of course lilies. When I bought the house where I live today I brought with me the first perennial that inspired my passion for gardening. It is the ming yellow day lily. Over the years I added many other varieties of plants to compliment the original perennials.

A couple of years ago I was looking at this garden from a distance. It had become unbalanced and overcrowded. It had lost its appeal and was in need of restoration. But I procrastinated and delayed. I tried to find ways to get around the tedious and difficult task of restoring this garden. Part of the reason I procrastinated was I didn't know what I needed to do to restore it. I knew many of the plants needed to be divided and the shorter ones needed to be transplanted towards the front. I had been adding plants over the years where they were not thriving and some of them needed to be planted in a better location.

I should have counted how many times I stood at the edge of this garden silently looking at it. The summer began to wane and I knew time was running short if I was going to do anything before winter, but the answer did not come. Time and time again I would stand looking at this garden trying to figure out a way to restore it to the way I envisioned it when I originally planted it. Then one morning I was walking around the garden, poking at a plant here and there, pulling stray weeds, and dead heading spent blossoms. I was still trying to figure out the dilemma of how to restore it. I stood back and took a long, hard look. The dew was fresh on the lawn and garden, which magnified the colors of the flowers. They were opening to welcome the morning sun (some of these flowers close up in the evening) and the greenery of the trees behind the garden provided the perfect back drop for the flowers. So there I silently stood, still not sure of what to do. What did this overgrown garden need to bring balance to it? I considered moving it, getting rid of it all together, adding a rock wall or perhaps I could bring in another feature that would bring new life to it.

Suddenly the answer came and I knew what I needed to do to bring new life to this perennial garden and restore the balance in it. The plants needed to be transplanted in the order of the colors of the rainbow! Starting at one end, gradually moving to the other end of this semicircular garden, the colors of the flowers would range from red to orange to yellow to blue and to purple with pinks and whites added to make the transition gradual. Of course the green of the foliage was the main theme to tie it all together. All the times I stood silently looking at my overgrown and tired old garden and finally the answer came. So I got to work and began restoring that big old garden.

My favorite garden these days is my water garden. This has truly been an effort and labor of love over the years. It is difficult to bring balance to the ecosystem of a manmade pond. Over the years I battled with algae and erosion from the soil where it had not been banked properly. I battled with leaves and dirt that blew into the pond. Finally, after ten plus years of trying many types of things to bring balance to this pond, it is clear, fresh and balanced. Today it brings peace, as a kind of silence to the soul. The fish in it are thriving as they surface and wait for an insect to come along. The exclamation mark to this labor of love came when snails naturally appeared at the edge of the pond. Now I can sit by the edge of the water garden and allow the quiet stillness of it to bring peace, balance and restoration to me.

Psalm 23 has been a long time favorite for many people. It is most often read at funerals and is one of the most frequently quoted chapters in all of Scripture. Entire books, Bible studies and even ministries have been based on this Psalm. Over the years when I read Psalm 23 it to ministered to me in different ways. If you are familiar with it, perhaps you could say it has been that way for you too. The verses that stood out for me most frequently were verses 2 and 3, "He *makes* me lie down in green pastures, he *leads* me beside still waters and he *restores* my soul." This Psalm is framed in the context of the life of a shepherd as they were in Old Testament times. Whenever I read these two verses I get a sense of trust and security that come over me. The peace and quiet my soul yearns for brings silence and balance to whatever is causing unrest at the time.

Everyone has a need for peace, security and balance in life. Part of this is having silence in the mind, will, and emotions. It can be interesting to see the ways a person tries to find balance in their heart and soul. It reminds me of when I was struggling with how to restore my big old perennial garden. Let's take another look at Psalm 23. The psalmist is aware of what it takes to find the type of balance in life we all crave and need. The first element needed is to have a relationship with the Lord. The Psalmist makes a relationship with the Lord as the shepherd of his life a priority and this is why he bookends Psalm 23 with *the Lord.* This indicates that the Lord is the most important person in the Psalm.

Once we realize that we need to follow Him, we can begin to understand that as our shepherd, He will provide protection, security, peace, silence and restoration to the heart and soul. Out of those elements comes balance, not only in relationships, but in all that life embraces. As the shepherd provides green pastures for his sheep, so does God provide for us. The shepherd does not necessarily force his sheep to lie down, but he understands the needs of the sheep and knows that through giving them green pasture they will follow their instinct to want to lie down and rest in it. The shepherd leads his sheep to quiet waters. This automatically brings an image of a quiet and peaceful scene of restoration. And the whole picture of the shepherd with his sheep can be summarized as one of being quiet. In other words, it is a silence that surpasses human understanding.

Silence and quietness automatically brings rest that is so often elusive. Sitting before the Lord in silence will bring peace far beyond what standing in silence at the edge of a flower garden or sitting at the edge of a quiet water garden when the ecosystem is balanced. When I ask a coaching client what peace is, the answers vary. But some of the words they use to describe peace are security, protection, silence, harmony, balance, quietness and stillness. Unfortunately, most people stand at the edge of their garden of *peace* and try all sorts of other ways to bring balance to their lives. They don't understand that the answer to having balance and restoration is through a relationship with Jesus. Bringing peace and balance to life means being silenced and allowing the Lord to minister to the soul just as the shepherd does in Psalm 23. To bring real peace, the deep, restorative work of the Lord needs to happen. What better way to find balance in life than by being silent, allowing the Lord to provide green pastures and quiet waters.

Where in your life do you feel out of balance?

What have you tried in your life to bring balance?

If you could have green pastures and still waters, what would those be?

Silence is the key word to finding peace, balance and restoration in life, what activity would help you when it comes to spending time in silence?

The Quiet Waters of Silence

Come sit in silence beside the quiet waters I am leading you to. Enjoy the green pastures I want you to lie down in. The water and the grass I am offering is that of my protection, security and love. I know balance in life is not easy when there are so many distractions. When pressures, priorities and idols create a distorted life, I am available to bring life back to balance. I know the world is full of ideas of how to balance life. Those ideas may work for a time, but gradually peace and quietness of the soul will once again become overgrown with the same old worldly difficulties. I invite you to a time of silence where you can sit in the green pasture and rest beside quiet waters, where you can regain the balance your soul longs for. As you sit in silence, be with me, your shepherd. Allow me to provide what you need and let me lead you. I want you to be restored and renewed. As the shepherd of old did it for his sheep, I want you to have the same. Do not wait until you faint and need to be revived. I offer the stillness and quietness that brings peace and balance to life the way no other shepherd can. My waters and green pastures are in the form of unconditional love, the promise of an abundant life and the security of eternal life. Sit down and rest in silence. Reflect on who I am as your shepherd and enjoy the safety, security, and peace and balance in life I offer.

Silence and Responsibility

For if you remain silent at this time relief and
deliverance for the Jews will arise from another place,
but you and your father's family will parish. And who
knows that you have come to royal position for such a
time as this?
Esther 4:14

This may not be a Bible passage a person usually memorizes. In a series of reflections on silence, it may seem odd to have a verse about speaking up surface. I happen to love this verse! My favorite part is "Who knows that you have come to a royal position for such a time as this?" When I was studying the book of Esther, I was desperately searching for God to do a mighty and miraculous work in my life and in the lives of the people I love. I wanted to see God's sovereignty at work and I was willing to take on whatever responsibility He wanted to give me to see this accomplished.

There are Biblical scholars who don't believe book of Esther should be included as the inspired word of God. Do you know why? It's because the name of God or Yahweh is not said once in the entire book. This book, when read at face value would appear to be simply a story of the Jews being in trouble again, faced with being killed to the point of extinction. Through a series of crazy and unpredictable events a Jewish woman, by the name of Esther saved her people just in the *nick of time*. This is a true story and even today, the Jewish people celebrate this deliverance in the Festival of Purim. It is a wonderful story of deliverance and is a rich and pivotal time in Israel's history. But as I learned in my study of this book, there is a whole lot more to it and is still appropriate for today. God's demonstrated his sovereignty and faithfulness to His people and this is the central theme of the story. When Esther took personal responsibility for her people, God's will was accomplished. If you have not read the Book of Esther yet, I would encourage you to do so.

What if Esther had not gone to her husband, the king? This was risky stuff, even though they were married. Esther was under his authority even though she was the Queen. As the story unfolded, Esther continued to be silent, much to her Uncle Mordeci's dismay. The clock was ticking. This is real life and the question often is to remain silent *or* to speak up. How many times in life does this question come up? Should I say something or not? If I do, will I screw everything up? Will I make matters worse? If I say something will I look like a fool? Will I face rejection? (Esther faced the possibility of being killed!) Am I doing the right thing? And so the ultimate question continues to be "Do I remain silent or not—for such a time as this?"

I was faced with this exact question a number of times in my life. Here is an example. When it came to the point where I had to deal with the abuse in my marriage I finally said to myself "If I perish, I perish" (Esther 4:16). I knew I finally had to speak up and do something, for the sake of my children. I was desperately searching for God's will in the Scriptures during that time. There came a point when God clearly told me to make *a generational change*. I knew it was time. I finally knew that I was being called to take responsibility and I did a scary thing.

I left my husband and took my two little boys with me. God's sovereignty and faithfulness was evident the whole time. It was such a big and overwhelming call, all I could do was follow God's command, be responsible for whatever was put in front of me and allow Him to work out the details of my deliverance. I overcame all my fears and I was finally delivered. It took years for me to be restored from the abuse in my life. Today I am entirely delivered of post traumatic stress and even though the scar remains, it is only a reminder to me that millions of people are faced with abuse of all sorts every day of their lives.

One morning, several months after my second husband left, I experienced God's sovereignty and faithfulness like I never had before. Words can't really describe what happened. It was of those *you had to be there* events. It was a crystal clear icy blue winter morning. As I walked to the mailbox I marveled at the hoarfrost covering everything. It was as though I was walking through a magical fairytale kingdom. Everything was white and glistening with frost. Even though it was icy cold, the sun was warmly beaming in a perfectly blue sky. But these days my heart was so heavy with pain and humiliation, I had all I could do to trudge through the everyday tasks needing to be done. On my way back from the mailbox a voice said to me "You are the queen of your domain!" What? Where did that come from? I certainly did not feel like a queen.

Faced with being divorced not only once, but twice, left me with shame that was indescribable. My future was totally uncertain, and I did not know how I was going to keep my house or provide for my boys. Telling me that I was the queen of my domain was so far fetched! Was this God telling me something, or maybe it was a riddle or to just tease my imagination? Years later, I now know it was God's promise that He is sovereignty and would be faithful to me. The precious memory of that winter morning is still a source of hope and encouragement when I am faced with difficult circumstances.

I can relate to Esther on so many levels. For example, she wondered how to save her family and how to do the responsible thing even when it meant life would never be the same, or possibly end. She could say "If I perish, I perish" to the point of losing her life, house, earthly security and all the elements that keeping her in the state of homeostasis, even when it was not healthy or godly. I can go back and play the *what if* game. What if I had stayed silent? What if I had never left? What if I had never expressed my concerns? What if I . . . .

It has been said looking back is 20/20 vision. That is true. Sometimes it is so much easier to see God's sovereignty and faithfulness looking back than it is in the present. What secret did Queen Esther have that helped her to speak up when she did? What moved her to not longer be silent?

I believe there were two things. First of all, she waited for God. She was given divine wisdom and knew timing (God's, that is) was everything. Seeing how she prepared for each event, she paid close attention to detail. She did nothing based on emotion or out of compulsiveness. Secondly, she overcame her fears. When she said "If I perish, I perish" she was saying she was not even afraid of dying at that point. She knew her role in her kingdom as queen meant there was no room for fear or anything else that would hinder her in her responsibilities and God's calling for her.

To remain silent or not for such a time as this is a big question! God will act regardless of our flaws, fears, silence and stupidity. But can a person live with regret for remaining silent? It's a scary thing to think events in life can be changed by speaking *or* by staying silent. What if the time for you now is for such a time as this?

Do you have regrets about a time when you should have spoken up?

If you did, was the course of events changed by speaking up?

If you didn't, how could things have turned out differently?

Were people hurt or affected by not speaking up?

Sometimes by not being silent, it may be that a person is called to write, sing or act out of responsibility to God's will?

If speaking up is not where your gifting is, is there another way for you to *not* remain silent?

What keeps you in silence? Is it fear? Is it anger and bitterness? Is it discouragement and hopelessness? Is it that God's timing is not right?

What is more difficult for you—to overcome fear or to act out of wisdom?

The Regret of Silence

My daughter, Queen Ester, was my servant of deliverance. It is true; she was beautiful on the outside. But she also had the qualities on the inside that made her beautiful. She sought wisdom and did not act on her own behalf. She remained silent for as long as was needed. When she knew that all the events were aligned according to my plan and that she was placed in her position for such a time as that, she did not hesitate. She overcame her fears and knew she had a higher calling. I ask the same of you. You are kings and queens of your domain and I ask you to seek divine wisdom. I ask you to overcome whatever negative emotions hinder you and keep you in silence. I ask you to recognize my power and sovereignty. I do not need your help, but I want you to be available to take whatever responsibility I give you. I know you cannot see the future. That is left to me. But rest assured I have plans and they include you. You are my workmanship, created in Christ Jesus to do good works, which I prepared in advance for you to do (Ephesians 2:10). Seek wisdom, overcome your fears, wait for my perfect timing and remain silent until the appointed time. Trust me, there is a purpose for you and all I ask is that you remain obedient as my servant Esther was. Trust me, the day will come when you will be able to say, "I am in this royal position for such a time as this."

The Sanctuary

Have them make a sanctuary for me, and
I will dwell among them.
Exodus 25:8

This is the first time in the Bible the idea of a sanctuary is mentioned. Let's take a look at what is happening here. God is giving Moses instructions on how to make a place of worship for the Israelites where they could worship (Yahweh) God. The chapters following Exodus 25 give very specific instructions on how the Tabernacle was to be constructed. God's instructions were so explicit that nothing was left for men to design. There were even details included as to where the furnishings were to be placed (Exodus 25) and how the oil (Exodus 27) and priestly garments (Exodus 28) were to be put together. The tabernacle was basically a mobile tent for the Israelites to take with as they traveled in the desert after their deliverance from Egypt. Much later, Solomon built the temple in Jerusalem (1 Kings 6). Sadly the Temple was destroyed when the Babylonians took the Israelites into captivity (2 Chronicles 36). Yet centuries later it was once again rebuilt (Ezra 3).

In the New Testament we have the story of Jesus going to the temple in Jerusalem as a young boy (Luke 2:42-50). Throughout Jesus ministry the writers told of the times Jesus went to the Temple where He had several altercations with the Pharisees. The tabernacle and the temple were considered to be a place of peace. Because of this attitude of reverence and peace, it was meant to be a place to observe silence. The word sanctuary in Webster's Dictionary has several meanings. The first definition of sanctuary is a place of holiness and worship. The second meaning is a place of refuge and protection.

I live near a national wildlife refuge and frequently we have flocks of various types of birds flying through as they seek a safe place to land.

In recent years we have had a return of the trumpeter swan and it is truly a miracle to see and hear them fly overhead as they head to the wild life sanctuary and the other nearby lakes and sloughs. I have a passion for seeing to it that birds have a safe place to live in peace and safety. Some years ago I planted selected shrubs and trees that would attract birds and wildlife.

Today when you walk around my yard you will see bird houses of all sorts, nesting boxes and even a butterfly house. Inadvertently a little tree frog found one of my birdhouses to claim as a sanctuary. I put a small ornamental birdhouse in a planter outside my front door. It is too small for any bird, even the smallest chipping sparrow. But the other day a slight movement caught my eye as I walked by the planter. As I looked closer, there were two beady little eyes peeking out of the little house at me. I took another glance and then I was able to make out what was occupying the little house. It was a tree frog sitting, silent and still, perfectly blending in with the brown bark of the little ornamental house. Tree frogs change color to match the surroundings they are in and so are camouflaged. He had found himself a little sanctuary, a safe place of refuge. He could be at peace and watch the world pass by and not be seen. But there are predators that come along and try to steal and destroy eggs and the young from the bird houses. The red tail hawks swoop through, the raccoons raid the bird feeders, the blue jays and grackles harass the mother birds. Each tries to destroy the peace, silence and quiet of the bird houses.

Do you have a safe place to call your sanctuary? People who come to visit me tell me that I live in a sanctuary. Of course they mean that I have a place of a refuge, a safe place to be. There's an atmosphere of peace and quiet with numerous places to sit and enjoy God's creation. Having a safe place to live is important for me and it makes me sad when I learn of the many people who do not have that.

It can be difficult for some people to find a refuge, a sanctuary where they can experience peace and silence. Emotionally, physically and even spiritually there are people who don't have a sanctuary for their own. I found this to be the case as I worked with families who suffered from family violence or encountered people who suffer with addiction. In my physical therapy work I work with patients in their homes who are under the oppression of poverty. My heart aches for all these people as I see that their sanctuaries; their homes are not safe places. The silence is never there and most of the time it is the basic need for survival that keeps these people going.

Whether the tabernacle, the first place of worship, the temple in Jerusalem Jesus visited, or my birdhouses that need regular care, these sanctuaries and the sanctuaries of our hearts are vulnerable to losing the safety and silence God intended for them. Just as I need to continually clean bird houses, put food out, chase the predators away and fix the broken bird houses to keep the sanctuaries for my birds a safe and peaceful place, so it is with the heart.

The heart is the inner sanctuary of the soul. It becomes a safe place when it is filled with the right things. When you look at what happened to the Israelites after God gave them orders to build the tabernacle, the next thing they were doing was making a golden idol to worship! How was that going to work into experiencing peace and reverence in silence in the tabernacle? It didn't. It is the same thing with the sanctuary of a person's heart. The heart needs continual attention. It is only through the restorative work of the Holy Spirit a person can keep the heart a safe place, one of peace and quietness. Only through repentance, forgiveness, showing love and kindness, prayer and time for solitude and silence can the heart can be restored to be a safe place again. It then becomes a sanctuary where the love of Jesus can be experienced and can be a place of peace and silence.

The blessing my pastor gave at the end of each Sunday morning worship service when I was growing up was exactly the same every week. As a little girl it was my favorite part of the service, not just because it meant that church was almost over, but because it gave me *goose bumps* to know that God was blessing me. It is known as the Aaronic benediction. Moses' brother Aaron was the first high priest in the tabernacle and God gave this blessing for Moses to give to Aaron. He says in Numbers 6:23 "This is how you are to bless the Israelites. Say to them:

> The Lord bless you
> and keep you;
> the Lord make his face shine upon
> you
> and be gracious to you;
> the Lord turn his face toward you
> and give you peace."

What is the sanctuary of your heart like? Is it one of peace and silence or raging with fear, anger, bitterness, pride, rebellion or depression?

What do you do to make your heart a sanctuary?

Do you surround yourself with godly people and attitudes to provide a safe place for yourself and your heart?

What keeps you from experiencing peace, silence and quiet in the sanctuary of your heart?

Would you like to have the love of Jesus, the blessing of God the Father and the restorative work of the Holy Spirit fill the sanctuary of your heart?

Silence of the Sanctuary

I commanded Moses and Aaron to build a sanctuary for my people, the Israelites. I wanted them to have a place to worship, to bring their sacrifices and to pray to me. This place of worship was for me alone. There were to be no other Gods. But they did not listen. Instead they chose to worship gold. The false worship of idols has been repeated time and time again in history. The sanctuary is to be a place of silence, of reverence and respect and a place of peace. This is also true for the sanctuary of your heart. All I want from you is for you to worship me from the sanctuary of your heart. But so often the heart is not a place of silence and peace. Rather it is raging a war against the world (Jeremiah 5:23). I want you to know that when you come before me and give me your heart, my love for you is the only thing that can silence the heart. Once the sanctuary of the heart is silenced from the world, then you can praise me and worship me and adore me (Psalm 30:12). So come to me and let me help you. Let my Spirit come into the sanctuary and silence all that torments you. Let the Spirit replace the torment with silence and peace so you may experience true worship in the sanctuary. Silence in the sanctuary of your heart will bring you to sing your praises for me, your loving God.

Serving in Silence

Lord, who may dwell in your sanctuary? Who may live
on your holy hill? He whose walk is blameless and who
does what is righteous, who speaks truth from his heart.
Psalm 15:1-2

As you look at this verse you may be wondering to yourself "Where is the silence in this?" This verse continues with the theme of dwelling in the sanctuary, although it doesn't say a thing about silence. Psalm 15 was written by David as he gave instructions to the people on how to access God in the temple. He doesn't say anything here about reverence or about having an attitude and heart of peace. Instead he uses words such as blameless, righteousness and truth. What does this look like in a person's life worship life? What does worship have to do with silence?

A number of years ago I had the opportunity to go on a short term mission trip to help in Texas to help in communities that had been ravaged by the hurricanes. We were there to help rebuild houses, to encourage those who were suffering and to minister in any way we could. It was one of those life changing experiences and it entirely changed my perception of worship. We prayed for the Holy Spirit to be with us during this time and there were a number of times when it was evident this prayer was being answered. There were three significant times of silence during this week long trip and each time became an act of worship.

One of those times was one morning when the hammers and saws were quiet. Several of us were working inside the house painting, plastering, scrubbing, caulking and doing various other tasks. Usually everyone would be chattering and talking and maybe even laughing. But at one particular moment everyone was silently working. It was a profound moment of serving in silence. Each person was doing what needed to be done. And each worker in their own way was worshipping by serving.

The second time of silence and worship was on the last day of our trip. The work was finished and we wanted to say goodbye to the family we had helped. We weren't sure how many family members there were because several generations were living together. We knocked on the door and asked Mary, the grandmother, to bring her family out of the FEMA trailer parked behind the house. I will never forget the look of love and peace in her eyes as she answered the door. I spoke with her for a brief moment and it was as though I was looking at the face of Jesus. It reaffirmed my experience of serving as an act of worship. In the next few minutes the entire family emerged from the trailer. Then all of the workers and the family came together forming a big circle and held hands. It was an intermingling of different cultures and ethnic groups and it was a sight to behold. It was extremely muddy as it had rained a lot during our time there. We were of different ethnic and cultural backgrounds, but united for a time of worship. We bowed our heads and stood together in silence before we prayed a prayer of blessing on the family. I knew the Holy Spirit had anointed this trip as His presence was evident in this brief moment of silence. We were in the sanctuary of God's presence doing a blameless and righteous act of serving. This was an act of worship.

The third time of silent worship came on the trip home. We were driving at night along the top of the western ridge of the Ozark Mountains. It was very late and we were singing, a bit giddy from lack of sleep and too much caffeine. It was a beautiful and clear night. Little by little a full moon emerged, peering over the top of the mountains. It was so awesome that it made us stop singing our silly little tunes and for a brief moment it was perfectly silent as we marveled at the beauty of what God had created. I wished others could have been with us to see and experience God as He put the exclamation mark on this mission trip. It was worship as I had never experienced before and once again, silence that was indescribable made the experience a supernatural act of worship.

We live in a culture where silence is not normal and even when we worship in our churches these days, a time of silence is rarely observed. Worshipping God can be done in a variety of ways. It can be through serving others, working, singing, writing, leading and doing what we do in daily life. As David describes, anything we do which is *righteous and blameless* is an act of worship. I have found that having a time of silence with any of these activities allows the Holy Spirit to work. It allows him to anoint me and become a part of the worship. As the prophet Zechariah said to the Israelites during a time of restoration for them after the Babylonian captivity: *"Be still before the Lord, all mankind" (Zechariah 2:13).*

How do you worship God in your daily life?

Do you view your body and your life as a sanctuary for the Lord?

Do you *worship* in silence or do you whine and complain when you work?

Do you brag about what you do when you are doing an act of worship?

How would your worship experience change if there was silence during at least part of it?

Acting in Silence

My servant David wanted the sanctuary of the temple to be a holy place. He told his people to lead blameless and righteous lives. And the same is true yet for today. As your life and all you do is an act of worship and a living sacrifice to me, do it in silence. Observe silence when you speak. Observe silence by listening. Observe silence when your heart needs restoring. Many aspects of my creation are silent. It is the way creation worships me. Take time and be sensitive to when silence is needed. Put aside the things that are non productive to worship and do not belong on the holy hill. Bragging and boasting, complaining and whining, ungodly speech can all be replaced with silence. In the silence check the condition of the sanctuary of your heart. Make the sanctuary of your heart a holy dwelling place. As your heart becomes a holy sanctuary, you will see the face of Jesus in the people you help. Your heart will be upright and blameless (Psalm 101:2). You will see as you worship me in silence and as you go about daily life that the Holy Spirit will anoint and bless what you do. And as you do this, you will in return also be blessed.

Power in Silence

I have seen you in the sanctuary and
beheld your power and your glory.
Psalm 63:2

I plan to meet King David when I get to heaven. I think we have things in common and I really want to talk to him about what was going on when he did a lot of his writing. Psalm 63 was written during a time when David was in the desert. He was being hunted and oppressed by enemies and wanted to feel God's presence of solitude and silence. His enemy was Saul, who betrayed him and was extremely jealous of David being given the crown of king (1 Samuel 18). David was hiding out in the desert of Judah, which was very rocky and dangerous. Here in a place where he didn't how things would turn out David wrote Psalm 63 as a reminder of God's presence. He was affirming that God was not silent, but was very real and present. David worshipped God in the temple and was reminding himself that he had experienced God's power and glory at other earlier times.

When a person doesn't think God is present that person is in a terrible hole. Thinking God is silent and not available comes from Satan, the enemy. This lie becomes bigger when a person is struggling with isolation, exactly what David was experiencing. The hole of darkness and perceived silence from God can come from a variety of experiences. It happens when a person is physically, spiritually and emotionally weak and for most of us we experience this more than once in life.

A time when I experienced the desert of God's silence (as I perceived it) came when I was spiritually, emotionally and physically weak. I had spent a season in surrender to God. It had been difficult and this season had been a lot longer than I anticipated. I had put God on a time limit, trying to control Him. I needed a new vehicle and it seemed as though it was in the shop every week.

Then, I lost my job. I was depleted in every way and to top it off, I had left my church and was worshipping at a church that was very good, but nevertheless, I was a stranger there. I was in a dry and weary time of my life. Depression set in and I couldn't get a handle on it. I stopped reading my Bible and lost interest in the outside world and lost my perspective on reality. I stopped reminding myself of all the goodness God brought to my life. I convinced myself God was not only silent but that He had abandoned me. And that is when I discovered what is at the core of depression. It is an unexplainable feeling of hopelessness. It is so deep and dark that it completely overtakes the mind, will and emotions. My heart began to shut down and nothing helped.

Of course, God was not silent. He was hard at work, and it wasn't that He was being silent. He was allowing me to experience what millions of people have gone through and deal with every day. Much later, after the fact, during a time with the Lord I asked him why He allowed me to go through such a feeling of hopelessness. His reply was that He wanted me to know what it is like to experience depression. Then I understood. Dealing with an episode of depression would make me more sensitive to those who also struggle with it. God allowed this feeling of hopelessness to come over me so I could get firsthand experience of what it takes to be restored when a person has been in the black hole or dry desert of depression.

There is one profound truth we need to always remember. *God is never silent!* King David was in the desert where he was hearing only silence. But he was relying on one of his other senses as he said "I have *seen* you in the sanctuary". Even though the silence in the desert was intense, David was relying on the fact that he had *seen* God's power firsthand. If David had not spent time in the sanctuary he may not have been able to bear the intense silence in the desert. Was God not out in the desert with him? Of course God was. David was eventually delivered and went on to become a great king. David's genealogical line shows he was an ancestor to Jesus.

God showed His power in my life after the depression. He provided me with a new job and I was able to buy a new car. The time of surrender became a sweet time of rest and God provided incredible worship experiences for me at my new church. *God is never silent. He never leaves, abandons us or rejects us.* But if we can remember the times of *seeing* His power and faithfulness in our lives, the black holes of darkness are easier to get through.

What have the desert experiences of perceived silence from God been like for you in your life?

Have you ever had an experience of seeing God's power in the *sanctuary*, from where you could draw hope and strength?

When God appears to be silent, what do you think He is doing?

What step can you take to experience God's power to help you through future times in the desert?

When you cannot *hear* God in the silence, what can you *see*?

I am Working

    My dear servant, my silence is not because I am not present. One of my attributes is that I am omnipresent. I am present everywhere, all the time. During your time in the sanctuary you will experience my power and glory. Store it in your heart. Keep it in the forefront of your mind and keep my power and glory available to give you strength when you are thirsty, weary and longing for deliverance. I want you to experience me in every way and if you only hear from me you will never actually see my power and glory. The darkness of depression and hopelessness comes as a thief and I will not deny that it is real. Even my faithful servant Job thought that I had become silent as he fell to the depths of darkness and hopelessness. But rest in the fact that if you spend time experiencing my power and glory, it will be an additional strength and resource for you. You may perceive silence as rejection, but there is power in it. Mere earthly humans use silence as a method of rejection, but this is not what I do. I am holy, all powerful and my love is better than life. Come to the sanctuary of my presence and experience all that I have in store for you.

Silencing the Storm

He got up, rebuked the wind and said to the waves,
"Quiet! Be still!" then the wind died down and it was
completely calm.
Mark 4:39

This is a familiar story of one of Jesus' more famous miracles. Let's take a look at what is really happening here as we read about a true story of God's power and sovereignty. Jesus needed to get away from the crowds and decided He and the disciples should go to the other side of the Sea of Galilee which is about a mile long. It is situated in a basin in the Mediterranean region and is surrounded by mountains. Cool air from the Mediterranean Mountains blows down and clashes with the hot air coming off the lake, making sudden, violent storms a fairly common event. Jesus was probably exhausted as He had just finished preaching The Sermon on the Mount to thousands of people. He was sleeping when a squall, one of these sudden violent storms, came up. Suddenly the boat they were in was put at risk of capsizing. The disciples *were* frantic and woke Jesus as the waves poured over the side of the boat. As Jesus came to, He realized what was happening. All He had to do was talk to the storm and tell it to be still. In Mark's account of the story he recalled that the sea became *completely* calm. Jesus, in His infinite wisdom then asks the question, "Why are you so afraid?" And I am going to paraphrase His next question "After everything you have seen, why don't you have any faith?" The disciples had seen miracle after miracle and yet when this squall came up and their lives were in danger, fear overtook faith.

As I work and minister to people through a number of roles, I continually find people dealing with one single problem with a common theme. That number one problem is their struggle with fear. Fear is the opposite of faith. This Bible passage gives a poignant illustration of that.

I call fear a secret sin. The reason I call it that is because so many people live in such bondage to fear they don't even know they are operating in that realm. It is like being in a boat on a lake or sea where there are constant waves that never cease. In some ways a person gets used to the constant motion of the boat. Many people don't realize they are living in the constant *motion* of fear. Then when a big storm of life comes along, the fear magnifies. Only when the fear becomes unmanageable is the person finally able to acknowledge fear as a dominant force in their life. When the storm subsides and there is a return to calm water, the fear also subsides, but just for a little while. The memory of the storms of life and the fear that accompanied it lingers. It returns to a slow simmer, but never completely goes away.

Fear leads to anxiety and has been a secret sin in my life. In spite of God's faithfulness to me in the past, I still struggle with the silent and secret sin of fear at times. Even when I remind myself of God's presence and faithfulness to me through everything, I still doubt Him at times. This leads to fear, then to anxiety and then to ugliness within myself and the squall of fear versus faith continues.

Sometimes when I struggle with fear, I go back and recount how God silenced the storms of fear in my life. It would take pages and pages to write all these examples down, but here are a few times where God, in His power and sovereignty, navigated those storms and silenced my fears and anxiety. I was put on the waiting list to get into physical therapy school the year I graduated from high school. I prayed and persisted in staying in touch with the college. A month to the day before school started, I received a letter telling me I had been moved up on the waiting list and if I was still available, they wanted me to join the class beginning the fall semester. Over thirty five years later, I still have that letter. But there had been a fear/ faith struggle. Jesus could have said to me "Do you still have no faith?"

A number of years later, my husband and I started a business. Because I was seven months pregnant, many people told us that we were crazy. I tried to push fear aside, but it was there. The business grew and thrived and in the years to come it was God's provision for us. Jesus could have said "Do you still have no faith?"

As I fled with my two little boys to find a safe place to hide when I left the abusive marriage, God directed and guided me through every single detail, from finances to legal to emotional and spiritual support.

At the height of the ordeal He was with us in a beautiful place where we were able to silence the fear of abuse and begin the healing and restoration phase of our journey. During that time I rested in the arms of Jesus. But in later events Jesus could have said "Do you still have no faith?"

Many years later as I struggled with an inoperable, but benign tumor in my brain stem. God silenced the storm that was as much a spiritual threat as it was a physical one. He provided one of the best brain surgeons in the world for me. My family and I learned, as we went through this storm, that hundreds and maybe even thousands of people were praying for me and my family on prayer chains. I hope to meet all of them in heaven someday! Today the brain tumor has shrunk by fifty percent. The doctors had no explanation for this as it was their goal to only stabilize the growth of it. Jesus could have said to me "Do you still have no faith?"

The year following my brain tumor, my second husband left. It was yet to be the biggest storm of my life. Physical, emotional, financial and spiritual waves crashed in on my life and almost *took me under.* Yet God provided healing, restoration, renewed purpose, and the birth of the adventure of life coaching. In the eye of the storm which I could have compared to a hurricane at times, God silenced my fears. He gave me the opportunity to finish college, a dream I had for many years. He also brought me closer to my sons than I ever imagined. He led me to godly women who ministered, encouraged, mentored, cried and laughed with me. Jesus could have said "Do you still have no faith?"

The list could go on.

The lessons to be learned from this are—

1) At times everyone struggles with the secret and silent sin of fear. But fear does not have to take over faith.

2) The struggle can be a daily one and needs to constantly be taken to Jesus. The best part is we do not need to wake him up as the disciples did!

3) The storms of life will come and go. Sometimes they are like a good old fashioned summer thunderstorm bringing refreshment and restoration to the sun parched summer. Other storms are like the Mediterranean storms coming out of nowhere, but are short lived. At other times the storms of life are like a hurricane force

one. The storm goes on and on and one may experience the eye of it, then be thrown back into it with a tidal wave and the danger of drowning. But God is still in control.

4) Jesus is never sleeping or even silent. In Mark 4:41, Jesus asked the disciples about their faith. They were terrified by the sovereignty of Jesus and His ability to calm and silence the wind and waves. Surely God, who came to us in the form of the man, Jesus, and performed such a miracle, still has that capability today!

5) We have the ability to take authority over Satan who tries to instill that fear in us (James 4:7 and Ephesians 6:10-18). Our faith is strengthened with the help of the Holy Spirit.

His Word is filled with stories of his sovereignty through out both the Old and New Testaments. Faith can take over fear and it can be silenced once and for all.

Be honest with yourself, do you ever struggle with the secret sin of fear?

What kinds of *storms* in life magnify the fear?

Do you ride the waves of fear and faith to the point where Jesus would say to you, "Do you still have no faith?"

When the hurricane of life looks like it will sweep you away once and for all, what is the one thing you could do to replace fear with faith, doubt with hope and be encouraged that God will silence the storm?

Jayne Kane

The Storm

As I ask you to get in the boat with me, as the disciples did same centuries ago, please be assured I am not sleeping or silent. As the squalls and the storms thunder and roll, and at times the winds are of hurricane force I am in the boat with you. As you stand in fear and terror and wait for me to say to the storm "Quiet! Be still!" be assured that I am sovereign, more almighty than any storm and I can make any wave and the wind obey me! I ask you to replace fear with faith, doubt with hope and to live a life of encouragement for others. The storms of life come and go, but I will never leave you. I allowed the squall to nearly overtake the disciples and it made an impact on them, as it is written about by Matthew, Mark and Luke. I ask you to allow the storms and the silence of my power to make the same impact on you. See the testimony of your life and how I have been in power through it all to strengthen your faith. Use your faith as encouragement to others who are in a storm of life. Above all, acknowledge the secret sin of fear to me and allow me to wash away the fear with the assurance of my love and concern for you. Faith silences fear when I work miracles. Sit in the boat with me and allow me to take the helm. I can navigate even the most violent storms of life when my power is acknowledged. My Child, wait for me, be strong and take heart. I am The Lord! (Psalm 27:14)

Bittersweet Silence

Then the church (throughout Judea, Galilee and
Samaria) enjoyed a time of peace. It was strengthened
and encouraged by the Holy Spirit; it grew in numbers,
living in the fear of the Lord.
Acts 9:31

Last week I was looking at a mess on the edge of one of my gardens. A large bittersweet vine had taken over not only the arbor installed to train this vine on, but everything around it. Just a little botany lesson here: American bittersweet grows as a woody stemmed vine and can grow as high as thirty to forty feet off the ground. It has small pretty green leaves and produces seeds that have a bright yellow covering. In the fall, the seed pods split open and the result is a beautiful, unique display of contrasting orange and yellow clusters of colored pods that look almost artificial. These clusters are very attractive and are often used in floral arrangements.

As I stood looking up into the tree, twenty five feet up, I could see how the vine had become enmeshed in the tree it was growing on. It had been an attractive vine at one time as it trailed over the archway of the arbor which was the entry point to my woods. The entry separated the groomed and neat appearance (most of the time) of my lawn to the natural and random appearance of the woods lining the back of my property. It had overtaken not only the archway, but the fence, the tree, the perennials and everything else that was growing near it. Bittersweet is an oxymoron! It is pretty, attractive and yet invasive and in Europe is poisonous. Bittersweet is a silent climber, but still. I don't know how my bittersweet vine got so out of control. All of a sudden it was that way.

Granted, much of what we experience in nature is silent, but somehow this vine had subtly and silently gotten out of control. Perhaps it was the fact that it was slow to get established and took years for it to grow over the archway. Or perhaps it is because the small green leaves are attractive and blend in so well with the woods. But mostly I think it is because I wanted to have as much of the orange and yellow fruit from it as I could get for my fall floral arrangements. So I didn't keep it in check by regular pruning. It had grown out of control, the seed pods were too high for me to reach and I did not know how to get it under control. This all happened subtly and silently over a period of time.

Luke wrote the Book of Acts and in this book he wrote about the ministry of Paul and how the Christian Church got started. In the verse we have here, we can see that the church grew and enjoyed a time of peace. Peace and silence are synonymous. The church was free from conflict and as a whole, grew in its understanding and respect of the Lord. But if you study the life of Paul, who was a key figure in building the church to this point, you will see he was not always peaceful. In fact, Paul (known as Saul before his conversion) was a bitter and hardhearted man. He was so bitter that he was antagonistic, brutal and oppressive to Christians. Paul was notorious for persecuting Christians and he was not ashamed of it (Act 8:3).

As we study the life of Paul, there was a pivotal incident that changed his life. It came when the voice of Jesus stopped him dead in his tracks (Acts 9:4). He had a conversion experience and eventually his ministry about the sweet message of salvation spread to the far reaches of the known world. Talk about an oxymoron! Paul's deadly bitterness was transformed to a message of salvation. His bitterness was reversed by the almighty saving work of Jesus and the Holy Spirit. It was no irony that the Christian Church thrived and it was all because of the work of the Holy Sprit.

When I look at my prayer journals and think about people and situations I prayed for over the years, there are some unanswered prayers. Some of these unanswered prayers were the result of bitterness in people. Bitterness often happens slowly and silently. Little by little it grows. It begins with anger and unforgiveness and eventually it takes on a life of its own. Pretty soon it is out of control and it becomes hard to see where kindness and gentleness was because of the bitterness. Hard heartedness is a direct descendent of bitterness and there is a fine line between the two. Bitterness shows up in the lives of divorced families, in the way an addict talks, or how an abuser rationalizes his attitude and actions. In the church it shows up as stubbornness, unforgiveness, arrogance, self righteousness and in *religious* attitudes. Bitterness is silent but deadly. It creeps in and eventually destroys the sweet and miracle working power the Holy Spirit wants to bring. Bitterness can be one of those secret and silent sins. Eventually, if not kept in check, it will choke and destroy a person, whole families, and entire faith communities. Most of all it kills the abundant life God originally intended for His people.

I am going to have to get help to get my bittersweet vine under control. It will require someone to crawl into the tree, take heavy duty pruning shears and methodically remove the woody vines choking the growth of the tree. Paul needed the help of the Holy Spirit to *prune* his bitterness and he did indeed have bitterness and hard heartedness removed from his life.

We all need the saving grace and love of Jesus' blood and sacrifice and the power of the Holy Spirit to overcome the bitterness in of our lives. If we don't have that, silent and deadly bitterness will choke and destroy the life God wants to purpose us with. Overcoming bitterness may call for a radical pruning. It may call for being struck down as was the case with Paul. But with the love of Jesus and the power of the Holy Spirit, bitter can become sweet, discouragement can become encouragement and a hard heart can become like the heart of Jesus.

Where has bitterness silently crept into your life?

Do you see bitterness in your relationships?

How about in your family?

How has it affected your church?

Do you see it in your work place?

Have you gone beyond bitter to being heard hearted?

If the bitterness was gone, what would it look like?

What do you need to do to have these areas of your life restored from bitterness to a life of peace?

The Silent Vine

My servant Paul was indeed bitter. He was even one step further than bitter and was hard hearted. But I had a plan. My plan was to have an outpouring of the Holy Spirit come into his life. It was my plan to have Ananias minister to him. It was my plan to use Paul not in the realm of human imagination, but only in ways I could orchestrate. Paul's bitterness began silently as a seed leading to hard heartedness. He destroyed people. He destroyed my people, Christians who professed their love and faith for me. The seed of bitterness had been planted long before in the mind and heart of Paul. It silently grew and eventually got out of control. Who knows how this could have happened? What about you, my servant? I have a Paul-like ministry in mind for you. Is your bitterness causing you to remain unforgiving and stuck in anger? Is it keeping you entangled in the choking vine of addiction? Is it keeping you from being in relationship with someone who for all you know may be on this earth for a short time yet? Is the bitterness preventing you from living with passionate purpose? I ask you this because bitterness is silent and deadly. It can only be removed from the soul by the deep restorative work of my Holy Spirit and my deep, saving love that came when my son, Jesus died and rose for you. Take this opportunity and turn the bitter to sweet. Don't let your heart become callous and unfeeling (Psalm 119:70). Be kind, compassionate and forgiving (Ephesians 4:32). In your hard heartedness, allow me to work. But do not delay. Paul had a conversion experience and I will use whatever means I need to deal with bitterness and hard heartedness. The opportunity is now. Begin by knowing how much I love you and that I have great things in store for you. Bitter can become sweet if you come to me, your Loving God.

A Divine Appointment

We have this hope as an anchor for the soul, firm and secure. It enters the inner sanctuary behind the curtain, where Jesus, who went before us, has entered on our behalf.
Hebrew 6:19

Recently I was praying about an upcoming event when God showed me it would be a divine appointment. In the following days, I couldn't stop thinking about all the divine appointments God orchestrated for me over the years. The times of praying with my prayer partners, interviews for jobs, sitting with bankers for loans of all types, and the times of walking alone in silence are examples of divine appointments. These divine appointments were the result of prayer, seeking wisdom and discernment, time spent in silence, allowing God to unfold the plan and then watching God *do* what he does best. The Bible is full of examples of God's divine appointments. Moses had one when God came to him in a burning bush (Exodus 3). David had one when, as a shepherd, he was anointed to be king (1 Samuel 16). Daniel had one as he was saved in the lions den (Daniel 6). The list is almost endless. But the one thing most of these stories have in common is that the person who God has the divine appointment with spent time in silence (and solitude).

Many of my divine appointments with God have been during the times of silence in my own home. I call my home a sanctuary. It is a safe place for me and I try to create a welcoming atmosphere of comfort and security for anyone who visits. Many times I will walk around the yard and reflect on what it is like for the wildlife to live in my sanctuary. I smile when the squirrels and rabbits hardly run away. They have little to be afraid of. My heart leaps for joy when hatches of bluebirds or wrens flit around on the lawn with little fear of being caught. Even the chipmunks scamper on the front porch, knowing they are safe and free and have little to fear (especially since the cat is gone). The deer that wander into the woods behind my house are wary, but unabashed by the sounds of humans. Now, I admit I get frustrated when the rabbits get into the garden or the deer strip bark off of the trees in winter, but I have more than I need for myself. I receive so much joy from watching all of these creatures as they thrive and cohabitate in silence.

As I wander the grounds of my property or sit in silence with my Bible, I frequently feel the presence of Jesus. It comes mostly during times of silence. In the silence, I can focus on Him and the distractions that so often get in the way are removed. This is when silence is a gift and becomes a divine appointment.

When Moses constructed the tabernacle in the wilderness (Exodus 26) and Solomon built the Temple in Jerusalem (1 Kings 6) the most important part of the structure was the inner sanctuary, the most holy place. This is where the Ark of the Covenant was kept and it was separated from the outer sanctuary by a curtain. It was a safe place for the ark and it was highly revered. It was a place of silence and only the high priests were allowed in the sanctuary. The Tabernacle was to be a place where God *lived* with His people. In this the Israelites had a reminder that God was with them.

This was a central theme throughout the Bible, including the book of Hebrews. Hebrews 6:19 says Jesus replaced the high priests of the sanctuary and He is even greater than Melchizedek, the most famous high priest in the Old Testament. When we enter into silent worship and allow the presence of Jesus to be felt we are in a sanctuary of hope. It is a safe place, as the verse says, for the soul. In silence we can focus and feel secure. As the verse before it says "We can take hold of the hope offered to us and can be greatly encouraged."

There is so much value in silence. It sharpens the senses. It provides opportunities for God to work. Silence opens the door to the sanctuary of God's presence. And it is only in the sanctuary that true safety can be found. In our culture today, silence is difficult to find. To truly have a divine appointment with God, silence is critical. Silence is the opening to the sanctuary of God's presence and is a true treasure.

Try this little exercise. Sit in silence for as long as it would take to read this entire page.

How did it feel?

Did it bother you or did you find the silence unsettling?

If you could orchestrate a divine appointment with God, what would it be like?

Have you ever had a divine appointment, but did not know it at the time? As you look back, can you see that it had been orchestrated by God?

Would you like to have a divine appointment with God in the sanctuary of His presence right now?

My Appointment Calendar

I have a calendar that is completely open for divine appointments. I love having these times with you, when I can show you my power, love and faithfulness to you. Since I am all knowing, I can guarantee I will orchestrate opportunities, events and people to carry out these appointments. If only people could understand that in the time of silence and in the sanctuary of my presence this in itself is a divine appointment. My son, Jesus is now the high priest of the sanctuary in heaven and He is waiting for the opportunity to intercede for you. Grant yourself the gift of silence. Do it often and regularly. If you need to do it in conjunction with solitude, then grant yourself that too. In the time of silence you will be free to hear, see and feel all that I have for you. As you come to my sanctuary, know that it is a safe place and I offer security, hope and encouragement to see you through whatever is creating uncertainty and causing you fear. (Psalm 27:3). When you come into my sanctuary for a divine appointment, let silence surround you and set aside the outside world. Trust me, I always want to have an appointment with you. What does your schedule look like?

Silent Praise

*Proclaim the power of God, whose majesty is over Israel,
whose power is in the skies. You are awesome, O God,
in your sanctuary; the God of Israel gives power and
strength to his people.*
Psalm 68:34-35

I remember as a child, and perhaps you do too, lying in the grass in the summer, watching the cumulus clouds as they billowed and moved across the sky. There was something almost sacred as I laid there, sometimes creating imaginary images from the clouds, as they took on a life of their own. Perhaps the thing I remember and what impressed me the most was how silent those big clouds were. As they grew and changed and got bigger and higher I would try to compare them to the size of objects on the ground. Of course, in my childlike mind, I had no idea just how big they were. And for as big as they were, they were so quiet! Even today yet, sometimes as I sit quietly on my front porch, one of those big cumulus clouds will catch my attention. I still love to sit and watch the shape one takes and how it moves, subtly changing its form and silently moving across the perfectly blue sky. But when they become storm clouds, this becomes another matter.

I wish I could sit silently and praise God the way the white cumulus clouds do. But most often when I sit silently I end up complaining and pouring my heart out to God. He wants me to bring my problems to Him, just as any dad would want to hear his child's problems. But all too often, I use the silence to commiserate about my burdens and difficulties. King David wrote Psalm 68 as a song of praise. It is a song of God's power and strength and how God brings His people to victory. I love verse four where it says that God rides on the clouds. His name is the Lord and we are to rejoice before him. It then goes on to say God is a father to the fatherless, a defender to the widow and one who sets the lonely in families and leads the prisoners forth in singing (Psalm 68:5-6). No wonder He is called the Awesome God!

Just picture God riding on one of those big, silent, cumulus clouds, watching over his creation, taking care of all of it. Sometimes it is hard to see him amidst the horrible stuff of this earth. There are many days when a person can ask, "Where is God in all of this?" But more and more I am coming to understand that the question is not, "Where are you, God?", but to say "I know you are here God in the silence."

Zechariah, the father of John the Baptist who was a cousin to Jesus, was struck dumb when he questioned and doubted the angel who gave him the message that in his old age he was going to have a son. You can read about it in Luke 1. Zechariah had to go about his duties as priest by using sign language. The only way he could worship and honor God was in silence. So how does that work?

God not only wants us to worship with our lips, but also in silence. As a priest, Zechariah would spend time in the sanctuary of the temple in Jerusalem. This time of silence was a time of character building for him. He doubted the message Gabriel the angel was brought and so as a way to get Zechariah's attention, God (through Gabriel) caused Zechariah to become speechless, unable to talk.

Many years before as David was writing Psalm 68, he was praising God for being awesome. It is a visual Psalm, full of depictions of nature. It tells of God's power and majesty, which is what *awesome* is all about. Because of David's relationship with God, he understood the power and strength God brought to His people. This is a Psalm of triumph as the people marched to the temple. They obviously were not silent at this point, but nevertheless, this Psalm is a song of praise to God in both the sounds of praise and the silence of praise.

If there is one thing I regret, it is in my times of silence I spent too much time being like Zechariah, questioning God and telling Him to show me His power and ability. If only I could have been more like David, understanding God has already shown His power. All a person has to do is look at the clouds in the sky.

What do you do in the silence?

Are you more like Zechariah or David?

What evidence is there in the *silence of life* that God is indeed powerful?

As you spend time in silence, try praising God in some small way. What is happening as you do this?

What can you do to worship in silence more often?

Silent Worship

Come and sit at my feet in silence. Look up at me and silently give me praise for my power. Set aside the complaining, moaning and weeping and for just this time tell me of how powerful I am in your life. Tell me this even though the silence may be a vivid reminder of a battle you are enduring. Just as you lie and look up at the clouds and marvel at their majesty, look up and marvel at how much more majestic I am than the clouds. I am even more powerful than the storm clouds or the mountains where they come from. Praise me as I sit in my sanctuary, giving strength and hope to my people. Praise me as I am with orphans, widows, lonely families and the prisoners. I am sovereign in the silence. I want you to experience that. David's song was one of deliverance and hope. Understand what happens when I displayed just how awesome I am. Zechariah questioned my ability and power. If you have a seed of doubt, you too will be hindered in speaking of just how awesome I am. Praise me in the silence. In time, you too will sing a song of the display of power I have shown you from my sanctuary. Let your heart sing and not be silent as you say "Oh Lord my God, I will give you thanks forever" (Psalm 30:12). In the silence sing "Praise is to God, praise be to God, praise be to God, praise be to God . . . !"

Final Thoughts on Silence

Many times solitude and silence go together. In solitude you have may have the opportunity to experience silence, but this may not always be the case. It is my hope and prayer you will use your imagination and whatever God has put before you to experience silence to bring you closer to Him.

Find peace for your troubled heart.
Experience the power of God as never before.
See God in a new way, far beyond what you ever imagined or believed.
Rest in quietness.
Find balance in whatever season of life you find yourself.
Discover when not to be silent.
Experience sanctuary.
Be able to worship God the way He created you.
See God's faithfulness at work.
Take your secret sin to God (which is no secret to Him).
Work through any bitterness that has crept into your life.
Have a divine appointment with God.
Set aside doubt and unbelief.

SURRENDER

Surrender

As I speak with people about my personal journey of restoration and how God used the elements of simplicity, solitude, and surrender to bring me through His healing and restoration process the most common comment from others was about surrender and how this would be the most difficult one to go through. And for me this was true. I was so used to being in control of life and I surrendered to God only when I was at my wit's end and did not know what else do.

Learning to live a surrendered life to God has been one of the most painstaking parts of my spiritual growth. Piece by piece and little by little God has taken every aspect of my life, turned it upside down and inside out and then rebuilt it. The result was my focus completely changed and in the end completely surrendered to Him. Even as I am writing, He is still putting me through the refinement process and I suspect part of living a surrendered life to God means I will always have parts of life that need to be given totally over to Him for His will and purpose. I invite you to come with me as we meander along the path of surrender and see what God has in store for you. As you read, pray, learn and reflect on what it means to surrender, I hope you will come to understand that our God is one of love and that He only has our best interest in mind. So read on and enjoy the journey.

The Battle

All those gathered here will know that it is not by sword
or spear that the Lord saves, for the battle is the Lord's
and he will give all of you into our hands.
1 Samuel 17:47

As a child, the first book to impact me was a book of Bible stories for children. It was written for six to ten year olds and it had beautiful water colored pictures accompanying the stories. Even today, when I look at this book, I remember how those simple childlike stories from the Bible were beginning to form me as a daughter of the King. As is the case with many books, eventually they get put on a shelf or in a box, some of them to possibly never to be looked at again. For years the *Children's Book of Bible Stories* sat in a box and eventually made it back to my bookcase. I made fabric cover for it and it sat among the repertoire of other keepsakes and mementos I saved from days long ago. That is until one day when . . . .

I was working towards getting my life coaching certificate and the obstacles kept coming at me. Some of these obstacles included financial difficulties and ongoing conflicts at church sapping my energy. A friend wasn't feeling well and was keeping it from me, burnout on the job and addiction struggles with loved ones added to it. I was determined and committed to complete the certification training, but each week it became more and more difficult. I knew in my heart God wanted me to complete the training, but the outside forces and obstacles were becoming nearly insurmountable. It was clear the enemy, Satan, did not want me to be a life coach. I was becoming more and more weary.

Then one rainy, blustery Sunday afternoon in March I sat alone with God pouring my heart out. He gave me hope and insight for the journey. On this day I was particularly burdened by the struggle of addiction that had gripped people I love. If you have experienced addiction or have been on the other side of seeing someone struggle with it, you know what I mean. As I prayed to God about all the things that were going on, he said to me, "The battle is mine." I thought of the Bible story of David and Goliath I had learned as a child. I went to the book case where I kept the *Children's Book of Bible Stories*. As I sat and looked at the watercolor picture of David and Goliath, I asked God what this meant. Then He gave me a revelation: I am David and the monstrous obstacles I was facing were the giant, Goliath. When I asked God what the rock in David's hand was, He told me the rock was prayer.

Relief swept over me and I sat and wept as I remembered what God had just told me "The battle is mine!" Armed with prayer alone I knew I could overcome whatever giant was standing in my way. The battle was God's alone indeed. As I look back I see this was a lesson in surrender. Lesson number one for me in surrendering was to realize no matter how big the giant when given to the Lord in prayer, the battle becomes His. As I think back on that Sunday afternoon I can still feel the physical weight being lifted off of me as God took the battle from me as I surrendered it to Him.

The story of David and Goliath is a favorite Bible story for many people and it is rich with meaning and insight. It is a supernatural and miraculous story depicting God's sovereignty, power, goodness and might. The Philistine giant was arrogant, boastful and big. In 1 Samuel 17 we see David was only a handsome, young boy. It is noteworthy to see what happened to David before he approached the giant. David had resistance from his family and King Saul. And yet David knew he was being called to fight the giant. He recounted previous battles with wild animals that he had encountered as a shepherd and how God had been with him. When Saul's armor didn't fit, David set it aside and took a staff and five smooth stones. David was unfamiliar with the armor of Saul, but knew the power of the stones from how he had used them in the past.

So as an act of surrender, David set aside the armor, took the staff and five rocks, ignored the doubt and sarcasm of his family, friends and Goliath too, and surrendered the situation to God. You could call this a true act of faith. This is what surrender is all about. True surrender says "I have faith that when I surrender this _____ to God, he will handle it the best way possible." True surrender says "I will pray, and prayer alone is an act of surrender." True surrender is the act of giving God all the control and prayer is the act of being in relationship with God while He is in charge of the circumstance, person or whatever is being surrendered.

Time and time again I have to go back to the story of David and Goliath and read about the events leading up to and through the battle. The day I surrendered my battles to Him was not a one time event. Countless times since then I have had to give the battle to Him. My struggles were not eliminated on that Sunday afternoon, they were given to God to battle for me. And it seems as though when the battles come along, I frequently have to visualize David and Goliath as a reminder to surrender the battle to God and just pray.

Many books have been written on prayer and it is one of my favorite topics. But some time ago an elderly client of mine gave me a profound insight about prayer that made as much of an impact on me as any book ever has. This client had lost her husband at a young age, leaving her with four children to raise by herself. During that difficult season of her life she had been given an insight about prayer and she kept it in her Bible all these years. The little card said, "God answers prayer in four ways"

Not yet . . . .

No, I love you too much . . . .

Yes, I thought you would never ask . . . .

Yes and here's more . . . .

When we have the perspective of God as our heavenly father and prayer as the way of being in relationship with Him, surrender becomes much easier. As David got ready to meet Goliath, he must have had this understanding of God to have faith and insight to surrendering the situation to God. We all have Goliaths in our lives. But too often we don't use the weapons God has given us. We would rather try to wear armor that does not fit properly or listen to the negative comments of others around us. Surrendering in prayer requires an act of faith, but in the end it is where God wants us so we can witness the miracle and blessings He has in mind for us.

Is surrender hard for you?

What happens when you surrender?

What is the most difficult thing for you to surrender?

Who can you relate to most in the story of David and Goliath?

Is it David, Goliath, Saul or David's family?

What do you find yourself saying when you try to surrender to God?

My Battle

My child, as you see the image of little David and the giant, Goliath, in your mind, do you find comfort and hope? I was there for that battle, it was mine. David gave that battle to me when he picked up a slingshot and five small stones. He set aside the armor and ignored the comments from his family. Instead he recalled past battles and clung to how I had been faithful to him and once again surrendered to me. As he prepared for the battle with Goliath, he was in relationship with me. He knew the circumstances were bigger than life and he knew that the only way to win was to surrender it to me. His heart trusted in me and he did not lean on his own understanding (Proverbs 3:5). As you struggle with bigger than life battles in your life, my child, pick up the stone of prayer. Pick up a stone for each battle you need to surrender and for each one give the battle to me in prayer. As you give the battle to me, allow your heart to hear me tell you "The battle is mine!" When you see me take the battle and make it mine, allow your heart to have faith and surrender it. Whether it is a financial battle, a spiritual one, a relationship battle an addiction or any other battle, I can handle it. Surrender means taking a step of faith, but when you give the battle to me, you will witness my power and strength and you will know just how much I love you. David knew this and it is how he won his battles. Put the stone of prayer in your hand, sit back and rest in my love and you will know the battle is mine.

Strongholds

The weapons we fight with are not the weapons of the
world. On the contrary, they have divine power to
demolish strongholds.
2 Corinthians 10:4

Franticly I was searching. I was searching for something I couldn't quite put my finger on. I knew I was not quite right. I knew I needed healing and I was desperate to find answers. I would pray, pace, cry, scream, sleep, cry some more and plead with God. I felt weighed down and trapped. Life was a black hole and I couldn't see the light. Every day was more of the same and I felt like a robot going about the motions of life. Absolutely everything seemed out of order and I knew life would never be the same. I was numb and yet at the same time, felt the pain in a way I never knew possible. My faith was shattered. Hope was gone. Life was not worth living, I had no reason to go on and I felt I was not lovable or worthy of giving or receiving love. This is how I described my life and myself after my second divorce.

I had experienced emotional and spiritual healing after my first divorce. There had been a season of enlightenment and new understanding and helped me move beyond the victim mentality to *survivorship*. But as I have so often described this particular time in my life, explaining that healing is like peeling off the layers of an onion. Little by little and piece by piece I was able to experience wholeness and joy in a way I never knew possible. Round two came in the form of a second divorce and it was quite different. I didn't think there was help for me and I felt like I was a hopeless case. But God knows better. No one is hopeless in His sight and there is healing for everyone. God knows each layer of pain that is deep seated in each of us and it is His desire that we be restored to live an abundant life the way He planned in the first place.

As I struggled with the trap of hopelessness, uselessness and all the other *lessnesses* I could dream up, God was at work. During this season I would wake up to the alarm in the morning wishing the morning would never come. My alarm was set to the clock radio and one morning God's healing hand was upon me as the alarm went off. A Christian radio station was playing a song that was referring to healing rain. And it did rain indeed, not literally, but spiritually. Healing rain came in the form of a prayer and healing ministry tearing down the strongholds that were hindering me. Healing came through books God *planted* for me to read. And healing came through wise and godly people who had experienced healing in their lives and told me of their own personal stories of victory. The restoration process had begun.

So I learned about strongholds. Quite often we think of strongholds as a fortress and this is true. Strongholds protect us and keep us from harm. There comes a time when the strongholds are no longer useful. Strongholds result in a faulty belief system. Our belief systems are not always correct, especially when they come from the dark places of hurt, negativity, ungodly attitudes and the pain of living in a sinful world.

My own strongholds had been erected to keep me from feeling love, from being vulnerable to anyone and to keep myself at arm's length from being hurt again. So I struggled with depression and discouragement, over-independence, distrust and fear. As I began meeting with two prayer ministers, my job with their help and the aid of the Holy Spirit was to tear down the strongholds I had erected in my mind and heart. And then God demolished them. Through confession and repentance I took the strongholds to the cross and gave them to God. Through the process I discovered how the strong holds kept me from having intimacy with God. Once I confessed and repented of these strongholds, I then surrendered my life to the will of God for my life. The result was I had a restored relationship with Jesus and a new outlook on life found only when the Holy Spirit is at work.

Complete surrender to the will of God is impossible when strongholds have a grip. Strongholds will keep a person bound so freedom to experience the joys and blessings from God are not attainable. Oftentimes when I watch it rain I think about healing rain. Rain has a way of restoring the earth from the dryness and struggle of drought. I love the smell of rain as it hits the sun parched ground. Rain is the best example of restoration I can find of how God restores his earthly creation. The good news is God provides *healing rain* for the spiritual dryness that result of strongholds that have been erected. There was healing available for all the strong holds that had been erected in my life. Whether it is fear and anxiety, unforgiveness and bitterness, control and manipulation, false security, confusion, denial, or self-indulgence there is healing for all of it.

Because we are all sinful human beings we need to confess our sins from time to time. Strongholds are sins too, but a stronghold is a dominant force in a person's life which continually keeps a person from living a free and restored life. It never goes away and in fact can even get worse with time. With the healing rain of confession and repentance, the sweet love of Jesus, the kindness of our Heavenly Father and the divine work of the Holy Spirit, strongholds can be demolished. God provides the freedom and joy He intended for us. I know, because I experienced it.

What strongholds dominate your life?

If there was a coaching question you have struggled with in this book or if you left one unanswered, you may be struggling with a stronghold.

Do you think there may be layers of strongholds keeping you in bondage?

Are you holding onto these strongholds thinking that there is no hope or help?

Are you ready to confess and repent of these strong holds and surrender your life to the will of God?

What would God, your heavenly father be telling you about these strongholds?

My Healing Rain

    I bring the rains to earth to heal the dryness and restore all living things. I invite you to experience the healing rain of restoration. It comes in the form of confession and repentance of every stronghold you have erected. A part of you may be saying this is what you need to hold on to. It is in reality, keeping you from having the relationship with me that I desire and wanted for us. These strong holds might be there for self protection, but the truth is they are keeping you in bondage and are holding back your freedom to live in joy. They are the result of the work of the enemy. I want you to know that no matter what the stronghold is or no matter how many layers of strongholds there may be, none of them are impossible for me to heal. No matter how deep or how wide the wound is or how much of a scar there is, my healing rain can cover, heal and restore you. That was my plan when I sent my son Jesus to die for all the sins and the strongholds that ever existed. Come to me and lift your face to the rain. Feel the coolness and dampness. Come to me with confession and repentance. Bring your broken spirit and contrite heart to me (Psalm 51:17). Surrender your life to my will and allow me to bring freshness, renewal and restoration. Lose the strongholds and replace them with my love, the sweetness of my son, Jesus and the divine inspiration of the Holy Spirit. Just as the rain brings restoration, this is what I want for you. Believe me and surrender. The best is yet to come!

Obedient Surrender

"Where you go, I will go, and where you stay I will stay.
Your people will be my people and your God, my God."
Ruth 1:16

I was thinking about relationships as I sat on my front porch this evening watching the sunset. Of all the changes I experienced in life, the changes in relationships have been the most prevalent. The sunset this evening was one of those late summer ones with clouds filtering in from the west creating various images and hues of oranges, yellows and blues. Every minute or so there was a different cast to the sky and it was absolutely breathtaking. As I reflected on the people in my life who have come and gone, including those who have stayed faithful or died, it came to me that sunsets and relationships are similar. They are always changing and no two sunsets or relationships are alike.

I love the story of Ruth. The story contains drama, suspense and romance. But most importantly, God's sovereignty and Ruth's ability to surrender to His will is what the Book of Ruth is all about. Yes, it is a story of loyalty and love, but this is exactly what surrender in relationships is all about. Ruth was a true example of being obedient to God in her relationships. As Ruth made the decision to stay with Naomi, her Moabite mother in law, she was inwardly saying God was sovereign and in control. Ruth would give Him the power to rule her life and determine the outcome. Interestingly, I have a note written in the margin of my Bible in chapter 1:15 saying this is a key verse in the saga of events. Naomi, Ruth's mother-in-law is telling Orpah her sister in law to go back to her people and her gods where they had come from! So much attention is usually paid to the fact that Ruth was faithful to Naomi. But little is said about Ruth's mother in law. Naomi made the decision to not go back to the gods of Moab. Naomi is staying faithful to God while Ruth is staying faithful to Naomi!

What about this whole thing of surrender in relationships? It is complicated and difficult to understand at times. What does surrender look like when relationships are not godly or are unhealthy and dysfunctional? Ruth was given divine wisdom and had been called to be loyal and live in surrender to God for the outcome of circumstances in her life. Ruth was a widow living in a foreign land. She was eligible to remarry and had been given the okay by her mother in law to go back to living the life she knew before her husband's death. But Ruth must have sensed that God had a divine plan. And just as the sunsets come and go each night and rarely no two are alike, Ruth understood that changes in families and relationships come and go too. Ruth not only made the commitment to stay loyal to Naomi, but to not go back to a life style she knew at one time.

As you read on in the story you will see Ruth surrender her daily life to God through living in faith and obedience to Him. You will see how God orchestrates circumstances to not only provide for her, but provides in ways that would also bless her. The story has a sort of fairytale ending as she meets Boaz and they eventually marry. Then to top it off, they come became part of the bloodline of Jesus. Of course, living a life of surrender in relationships will not guarantee the course of events will go the way we want. But living a life of surrender in relationships means that God will bless us for our obedience and faithfulness.

What does surrender in relationships look like in your life? What about the grown child who moved back home? Or the elderly parent who needs constant care and attention? How about the boss who criticizes and is antagonistic towards having a faith in God? And then there is the spouse who abuses or is bound in addiction? No two sunsets are alike and no two relationships are alike. But the act of surrendering to God covers all of it. As I surrendered many relationships over time, the common theme of surrender in all of them was staying obedient to God. Through prayer, discernment and seeking His will in each circumstance and allowing God to orchestrate how He would carry out His will was the key. Of course, there have been many times when I rebelled at how God was operating or times when I thought God had forgotten about the relationship. But God is faithful and will always do what is best for me, just as He did for Ruth.

How can you relate to Ruth?

What part of relationship(s) is hardest for you to surrender?

When you are faithful and obedient to God through surrendering, what happens?

As you surrender your relationships to God for His will and purpose, how do you feel?

What one relationship is God calling you to especially surrender and lay at the cross for Him to care for?

Surrendering in Obedience

What is that you are saying, my child? You do not think that surrendering the person on your heart will change anything? Don't you understand and know how I am in charge of all that is around you, including the people you and I both know and love? I gave you Ruth as an example of living a godly life of obedience and faithfulness as the cornerstone for surrender in relationships. Staying faithful and obedient to me is to be foremost in surrendering the people you love. As you do this, you may be surprised at how your perspective, the person or the situation is changed. As you surrender, the gods that come along with that relationship must also be surrendered. Even if you are not aware of any gods or even when the person themselves is godly, check your own motive and perspective in the relationship. Make sure it is totally surrendered to me. As you surrender your relationships, you heart is staying loyal to me (1 Chronicles 29:18). Know that as sunsets change from night to night, the relationships in your life will also change. This is especially true when it is a surrendered relationship. The truth is you have no more control over people than you do over the sunsets. But I have power and control over both. Yes, I have given people free will which is one difference from the sunset. But I am still sovereign. Knowing this should give you comfort as you surrender. So the next time you watch a sunset, let it be a reminder to surrender the people we both know and love to me. And as you stay faithful and obedient to me, you will experience a surprise of blessings as Ruth did. She never dreamed my son, Jesus, would come from her bloodline.

Surrendering to Become Equipped

May the God of peace who through the blood of the eternal covenant brought back from the dead our Lord Jesus, that great Shepherd of the sheep, equip you with everything good for doing his will, and may he work in us what is pleasing to him, through Jesus Christ, to whom be glory for ever and ever. Amen.
Hebrews 13: 20

If you walk through the gardens lining my property, you will see that each one has a purpose. Of course, collectively they were planted to provide beauty and enjoyment. But there is another thing about them. Each one was designed and planted for a function. Over the years I collected various plants and flowers suitable and perfect for each garden. One of my favorite gardens is the hummingbird and butterfly garden. It was planted to attract hummingbirds and butterflies, each plant having a specific role in the garden. The trumpet vine sprawling up the lattice backdrop has bright orange tubular flowers and provides nectar for the hummingbirds. The butterflies love to sit on the orange butterfly flower and white coneflowers before flying off again. The red monarda and red magic daylilies are natural attractors and blue butterfly delphiniums add interest and natural beauty.

As a gardener I plant, water, weed, deadhead and mulch to provide the best possible environment for these flowers. My heart gives a little leap of joy when I see a hummingbird or butterfly land to get nourishment from the flowers. Sometimes as I stand and survey my gardens I think about how surrendered they are to whatever I do to provide for them. There are times when the weeds get ahead of me or when it starts to get too dry. And then I feel a little bad as I am not equipping them to do what I intended for them. But they continue to surrender and grow in spite of my occasional negligence. So much of creation is that way.

Sometimes surrendering is part of becoming equipped. This passage from Hebrews is exactly about *surrendering for the purpose of becoming equipped.* I wrote in the margin of my Bible alongside this passage: this is a message of hope. I would also call it the backbone of the gospel of the good news. The first part of this passage is all about what God has done for us, what Jesus was equipped to do and how He has equipped us. The second part of the passage is all about what we in turn are to do, as we are equipped through the saving blood of Jesus.

When we are becoming equipped we are to be surrendered. Just as gardens are surrendered to the care of gardener, so God's sheep are to be surrendered to Him. Becoming equipped can be an uncomfortable and painful process at times. It may involve going through a season of trials or tests. We may become equipped by going through a time when we know God is shaping and refining us. Oftentimes during this season of equipping we may question if there is a plan and hope for us.

If you take a close look at this passage, the key phrase in this is we are being equipped for everything *good* to do His will. At the beginning of this passage our God is defined as one of peace. We need to keep this as the central focus as we practice surrender. This is not easy as there can be many distractions and, of course, Satan wants anything but for us to surrender to the will of God and rest in His peace.

Being equipped means surrendering through faith, faithfulness, obedience and perseverance. It means believing that we have a God of peace who brought Jesus back from the dead. Becoming equipped means that we can know with full hope that He wants to work in us for what is pleasing (Romans 15:3-5). Even now, as I sit here writing, the struggle to surrender is huge. As I look out the window at the hummingbirds at the feeder, I feel like them. They are darting back and forth and batting their wings at each other, trying to keep the others from sitting at the feeder. So often I am more like the hummingbirds than the surrendered gardens they visit. Becoming equipped is hard. It is hard to sit still and allow God to do the deep work of restoration in the heart. It is hard to persevere when the outcome is uncertain. And it is hard to be obedient when a person's instincts are to bull nose ahead. So often I would rather do things my own way. But because I know that we have a kind and gracious God of peace who wants only good for me, I can have faith He will accomplish what He wants to equip me for in His own way and time.

When it comes to becoming equipped what is the most difficult thing about being surrendered for you?

Can you think of a time when you did not surrender to becoming equipped and it did not go so well?

What about a time when you allowed yourself to be surrendered to God's equipping you for His will and purpose?
Rate the four aspects of becoming equipped during a season of surrender from easiest to hardest for you:

Obedience   Faith   Perseverance   Faithfulness.

Becoming Equipped

    Do you know what I am doing, my sheep? Of course not. At the present you do not know what the outcome of surrendering to become equipped will be. You do not know the circumstances and events I will orchestrate. One thing you can be assured of is that as you grow during this time of surrender through obedience, faith, perseverance and faithfulness, you are becoming the person I created you to be. As you do my will from your heart (Ephesians 6:6), serve and surrender wholeheartedly. You will be able to accomplish through me what is good and pleasing. As you carry out my will you will be the message of hope and you will be able to minister to others who struggle with surrender and with becoming equipped. As you do my will you will bring peace and the message of my eternal covenant to others. You will find hidden blessings from this time of surrendering to become equipped. And one day as you look back you will say, "So that is what my God of peace was doing." Surrender to the message of hope and know as the great Shepherd of the sheep I want only what is good and pleasing for you. During this time of surrender keep this as your central focus. You will not be disappointed.

Abraham-like Surrender

But the angel of the Lord called out to him from
heaven, "Abraham! Abraham!" "Here I am," he replied.
Genesis 22:11

If you want to read a story of drama and suspense at its height, read Genesis 22. To find a little background information about the drama of this story, also read about how Isaac was born. He was a miracle in that Abraham and Sarah were very old when he was born. So if you don't know the story, I encourage you to read it in Genesis 20 and 21. I have often wished for the faith of Abraham. Time and time again God tested him. It is no wonder God made him the father of a great nation, the Israelites. The story of how Abraham took Isaac up the mountain to be sacrificed is truly a story of true surrender. It is easy for us to read it and give a sigh of relief as it became clear to Abraham that he did not need to sacrifice Isaac after all. We know the outcome in short order. But what about Abraham and what he went through during this ordeal?

To put the whole event in perspective, the journey to Moriah was about forty eight miles. That was a lot of walking and took a fair amount of time to make the journey. It also gave Abraham a lot of time to think about what this trip held for him. Some other facts to put this story into perspective were Abraham was over one hundred years old at the time and he loved Isaac *very* much. After all, he had been a miracle baby. Isaac was a young man by this time and was smart enough and also perceptive enough to ask where the lamb for the offering was.

So Abraham told his servants to stay back while he and Isaac trudged up the hill along the rocky path. Abraham's heart must have been so heavy and filled with emotion. Why would God ask him to do such a thing? Here is the key to Abraham's surrender. Faith and obedience were what motivated Abraham. That is what Abraham-like surrender is really all about. Abraham did not plead, whine, wring his hands, ask questions, bargain with God or complain. Instead he did what God told him to do. Abraham also approached this test from a practical stand point. He took wood with him and understood the sacrifice was going to be an act and time of worship.

I tend to surrender only when there is nothing else left to do. I surrender when I have tried everything I can think of on my own. It is only then when I give the situation or the person or whatever it is that needs surrendering to God. And I say "Here God, I can't fix it, maybe you can!" Even today yet, my prayer list is really a list of all the things I have tried to fix myself and now I am giving them to God. Sound familiar? I think God must chuckle, groan or both at times.

The event of sacrificing Isaac was truly a test of faith. We all are faced with tests at one time or another. Tests may come in the form of surrendering a child to the care of the armed services or through an intervention that will take a loved one to chemical dependency treatment. Sacrificing may come in the form of tough love when a spouse says "enough abuse or cheating" and it is time for change. It may come when a loved one is called away to another country to work or to go to school. It may come when the doctor says there is no more chemotherapy to try. Tests of surrender come when there is no job and the mortgage is going into foreclosure. It comes when a loved one goes to jail or prison or when an elderly person can no longer live at home. The list of tests is endless. They are as individual as each human being and they come in *clumps* at times. At other times the test may be the *smoldering* type of test that goes on and on with no ending time in sight.

God tested Abraham to solidify his faith. And so often this is the intent of the tests God allows each of us to go through. Tests requiring surrender require a measure of faith, if it is to be like the surrender that Abraham had. He was asked to sacrifice the most precious thing in his life and God knew it.

But here is the best part. God provided a ram for Abraham to sacrifice. In the end Abraham called this place "The Lord Will Provide." We too have a God of provision. It may not always be the way we want it to be, but he will never leave or forsake us. He will honor us for our faithfulness. At the time of testing, it may be difficult to see how God will use the test. Faith is all about believing in what cannot be seen.

God wants to bless us for our obedience, perseverance and faithfulness to him.

One side note about the test of surrender; temptation is not the same as testing. Testing comes from God, temptation does not. Only Satan will tempt. If you are faced with temptation, the way to deal with this is not to surrender to it, but to take authority over it. You can do this by saying, "In the name of Jesus, Satan, get behind me and go away." Then walk away from the temptation. In the end, God will honor you for this too.

What has been your biggest act of surrender in your life?

Did you surrender with wringing hands, complaining and bargaining or did you surrender as Abraham did, with a practical and matter of fact attitude?

In your faith journey, has there been a test that *broke* you?

What events or circumstances surrounded the test?

Have you been able to heal and be restored from that test?

If you have not, would you like to be able to be restored?

If you have not healed from a test, what is keeping you in a *broken* state?

Like Abraham

My son, Abraham, had the faith that a father of a great nation needed to have. Time after time I tested him and He never became bitter or broken. He understood that I am a God of provision and I desire to have my faithful ones be blessed. I asked Abraham to surrender his most precious earthly thing to me: his one and only son, Isaac. And even though the journey was hard and rocky and uphill, he did what he needed to do. I know that your own journey of surrender is hard and rocky and uphill too. I understand the test and I understand the temptations too. Abraham's faith was strengthened and he honored me by acknowledging that I am the God of Provision. I provided a ram in the bush in a timely manner, at the last second before the altar of surrender. Know that I am not only a God of Provision, but also a God of protection. If you are broken by the trial of testing, please come to me for healing and restoration, for I am a God of this too. It is not my desire to have a broken world, but one that has been restored and out of brokenness is living for me. If you are one of those, ask for the healing and restoration that will bring you to a new place of living out of that brokenness. I want you to have a strengthened heart (1 Thessalonians 3:13). My restoring act of salvation through the death and resurrection of my son, Jesus, is the way to healing the brokenness. As you seek healing and restoration, I will orchestrate events and people for you who have been restored through me. It is out of their brokenness that they can help others heal. I am a God of Provision and that includes providing for the needs of those who suffer. I am not the cause of suffering as many believe. But rather I am a God who suffers with his people. Tests and trials will come and surrendering is too overwhelming at times. But if you can be like Abraham and focus on worshipping me, you too will be blessed. And you will be able to honor me by calling me the God of Provision.

Oaks of Righteousness

But we also rejoice in our sufferings, because suffering produces perseverance, perseverance, character, and character, hope. And hope does not disappoint us, because God has poured out his love into our hearts by the Holy Spirit, whom he has given us.
Romans 5:3-4

What exactly is surrender anyway? We tend to think of it in terms of waving a white flag and giving up or perhaps coming forward with hands up as a gun pointed in the back. But today I received an insight that is much more beautiful than any of these images. And as a believer in Jesus, it is so fitting. Surrender is simply giving back that which has been given to us. When I think of it this way, everything has been given to me by God, except for . . . . suffering. Suffering is not of God or from God. We suffer because we live in a sinful world in desperate need of restoration to God. But suffering needs to be surrendered too. And I think suffering especially needs to be surrendered, because God in His sovereignty is the only one who can do anything about it.

There is a group of oak trees standing tall and mighty in the woods behind my house. These trees are a remnant of the virgin forests which covered this region over a hundred years ago. They are burr oaks trees, gnarly, tough and majestic. They stand over sixty feet tall and are more than five feet in circumference. I studied them a little and came to the conclusion that judging them by their size, they are 125 to 150 years old. Four of the oak tress are particularly interesting to me. They stand as though they are forming a square, with an oak tree at each corner. When I stand in the middle of the square of the oak trees and look up I can barely see the sky between the leaves. That is how big and stately this square of trees is. When I stood in the stand of oak trees recently,

I pictured Father God looking at them, saying "Well done, good and faithful servants."

These four old oak trees are a reminder to me of perseverance. They withstood countless storms, blizzards, high gusty winds, droughts, lightening and torrential rains. And yet there they stand, gently waving in the breeze, totally surrendered to the creator God. They have not rotted from the inside out, as is a common problem of these trees. As the squirrels do their acrobatic tricks and play in the branches of these trees, they continue to produce an abundance of acorns. These burr oaks stands as a true master pieces of character coming out of years of persevering. Through perseverance the trunks and branches of these trees were formed and strengthened. The storms made the trees stronger. If there was a weak branch, nature took care of *pruning* it to allow for more growth. These oaks surrender to the seasons each year. As I look at them on this late summer day, they are dropping acorns and doing their part to provide for the next season—winter. As they surrender they continue to give back to God what he gave them. The shade they produce covers the tender plants in my woodland garden. The acorns they drop are for the wildlife. Their deep roots prevent soil erosion and the leaves that drop in the late fall provide nutrients for the soil.

I am humbled to say that I have not always fared so well in my own perseverance and suffering. I have not always surrendered to the suffering and I don't always produce the things that godly character development should bring. I tend to get discouraged, depressed and anxious. Then fear sets in and then . . . . Well, God has to clean up the mess before I can persevere and allow the character development in me to produce hope.

As you read the passage in Romans chapter 5, take notice of the best part of this passage. We can have hope. This is where the focus really needs to be. It is not about how the suffering is going—as if suffering can go well! It is about the fact that God poured out His love into our hearts by the Holy Spirit. That is the difference between surrendered suffering and suffering that is not surrendered. When the Holy Spirit can be alive and at work in a person's heart, it prevents rotting from the inside out (like oak trees sometimes do). It allows grace to enter in and allows for righteous suffering.

Isaiah talks about suffering in terms of ashes, mourning and despair. But in the following verses he says (Isaiah 61:3) they will be called oaks of righteousness, a planting of the Lord for the display of his splendor. The result is righteous surrender in spite of suffering. As the oak trees are a display of splendor in my woods they are a reminder of persevered in suffering. As they persevered through the storms of life they were able to produce seasons of beautiful splendor. It took years and years to produce the characteristics which make them majestic and sometimes that is the case for us mere earthly humans too.

I recently had a physical therapy patient who is ninety nine years old, but you would think she is only in her seventies. As she told me bits and pieces about her life I thought about her inward and outward beauty. And when I learned of all the horrible things she has endured and suffered through, I thought of the oaks of righteousness. She is not *rotten* from the inside out, but rather the storms of life have formed her character so she is an inspiration to everyone she meets. She radiates beauty and she is truly an oak of righteousness. I asked her what her secret to living a long life is and she said hard work and accepting whatever happens. That is what righteous surrender is really all about.

As the storms of life have blown through your life, what have you done or not done to persevere?

What parts of your character have been developed through those storms?

What has given you hope?

Have you asked the Holy Spirit to pour out the love of God into your heart during suffering?

Can you look at an oak tree and say "I want to be an oak of righteousness too"?

The Giver of Hope

As you suffer in this world I would like to encourage you to persevere. I know that being in the world brings suffering and is more than my children should have to bear. But as you study the gnarly branches and the coarse trunk of an oak tree, also admire the strength and splendor of it. As it stands higher than any other tree, see how it surrenders to me. It is an oak of righteousness; a tree that gives hope that comes from suffering, from persevering, from enduring and from surrendering. This tree is part of my creation and in spite of the raging storms it has suffered through, it continues to live in splendor and majesty. I want the same for you, because you are also a part of my creation. I have demonstrated that by pouring my love into your heart (Romans 5:5). I have given you the Holy Spirit to help you with righteous surrender and in turn your character will grow and be strengthened. As you are strengthened you will be given hope and will give others hope. You too will be honored with majesty and splendor (Ephesians 6:8). You are my oak of righteousness and I love you for that. Hold onto this love, because that is what gives hope. Through the help of the Holy Spirit I am with you to help you with righteous surrender. Then you will know how much I love you and you will have hope. Surrender your suffering and persevere. Arise with character, hope, majesty and splendor like the righteousness of the majestic oak tree!

Casting and Surrendering

*Cast your cares on the Lord and he will sustain you; he
will never let the righteous fall.*
Psalm 55:22

I love to go fishing. I grew up fishing with my grandfather and
in later years my husband and I spent countless hours on the lakes
of Minnesota and Wisconsin fishing for our limit of fish. On one of
our trips I caught a trophy fish and it now hangs on the wall in my
den. It is a 15 pound, 12 ounce, 38 inch northern pike from Zippel
Bay on the Canadian border. Most of our fishing was for large and
small mouth bass, northern pike and whatever else that would bite
on the spinner bait we cast into the water. Thankfully I had patient
teachers who taught me the art of casting. We would launch our boat
and as quietly as possible troll around the weed banks and shores of a
lake. At first I could not cast very far. At times the bait would end up
getting tangled in the branch of a low hanging tree. Then we would
have to temporarily stop fishing and untangle the line before we could
continue on. This was frustrating at times, especially if it happened
when we knew there was a big old bass lying under a sunken log in the
water while my fishing lure was tangled in the tree above!

Fishing is considered a sport, but I also consider it an art. There is
a certain amount of expertise and knowledge a person needs to have to
be successful at it. There is also a certain amount of discipline that is
needed. It takes patience, perseverance and a general love of the sport
to be able to be successful at fishing. And there are many people who
would say that it takes *luck* to be successful at it. The casting part of
fishing is more active than the traditional pole and line type which
is passive. There are advantages and disadvantages of both types and
there is a time and place for each one, depending on what you want to
fish for.

There are many types of casting when it comes to fishing. The casting a person does when fishing on a quiet lake at sunrise or sunset is quite different from casting from a fishing boat at sea. And the casting that the disciples did with their nets is yet another form of casting. Webster's Dictionary has several meanings for casting. It can be mean to cause to move or send by throwing, to put forth, to throw away or to get rid of. When it comes to fishing, the fisherman (or woman) is getting rid or throwing the line with the bait attached in order to get something in return; hopefully a fish! And of course there are many times when you cast or throw something away, never to be seen again; such as the garbage.

As David was writing Psalm 55, he was surrounded by enemies. He was about to be seized and his very life was being threatened. He was being verbally and physically attacked and fear was the number one emotion overriding all of this. David found himself in these situations time and time again as he lived and reigned as king during tumultuous times. The Philistines were a powerful nation, constantly threatening the Israelites. And then there was Saul, who stalked and hunted for him (1 Samuel 19). Later there was Absalom's conspiracy which threatened the City of Jerusalem (2 Samuel 15). It seemed as though David was continually battling the verbal, emotional and physical threats of his enemies.

But David was a man of honor, faith and integrity (most of the time). As he wrote this Psalm, he intended it to be sung in the Temple. David was acknowledging what needed to be done to survive the overwhelming fear which was as much of a threat as anything. *Cast your cares on the Lord* is a command to surrender. David is not specific about what the cares are in his statement, so cares could be anything and everything. On the *bad* fishing days we cast for *anything* that will bite, just for the fun of it. So as David is commanding his people to cast their cares, he is saying *anything and everything*. Have you ever been involved in a conspiracy? It is messy, entangled, totally destroys trust in anything and everything and it can have long lasting negative affects. David knew what anything and everything meant.

So the command is to cast your cares on the Lord. At this point I envision Father God having very big shoulders. I can cast all my cares, big and little on him. What an act of surrender! But I know this is much easier said than done. In the act of casting, God wants us to throw our cares to Him, but unlike fishing, He doesn't want us to reel them back in. But oh how often do we try to do that? We give the care to God, put it on His shoulders and then reel it back again. So often I do it repeatedly. And then just as I do when I am fishing, the care gets tangled up in something and then I have a bigger mess yet.

What I love about this verse is that the word care is not limited to one certain thing. Cares can mean anything from the daily grind of time and financial management, dealing with family and work problems to the biggest, most catastrophic life threatening problems imaginable. Cares are as unique as the individual who carry the burden. And David isn't just saying "cast the care away" but he is practical about it and understands the care needs to go somewhere or it is not really getting rid of it. We are to cast the care onto the Lord, our Father God's big shoulders. It is one of the most intentional daily activities of restoration we can do. But it takes practice, intentionality and the help of the Holy Spirit.

The best part of Psalm 55:22 is in the second half of the verse. David, as a man of faith, knows and understands in his heart that God will sustain him. Time and time again, God won battles for David (2 Samuel 19). Personally as well as in his calling as a king, David repeatedly came through battles and was sustained by God (1 Samuel 19). Perhaps God allowed David to constantly endure battles as a way to remind him of his dependence on God, living a surrendered life. When a person lives in surrendered dependence on God, he will be empowered to live a life of righteousness as the last part of this verse describes.

Righteousness is not a word used much in today's language and it certainly is not a word I use in my daily vocabulary by any means. I don't use the word righteousness when I am working with coaching clients or ministering to others who are struggling with their faith in Jesus. But it is a word that really can not be ignored. Righteousness quite honestly means what is right, but specifically a righteous person is who honors God and orders their lives in all things according to God's will (Romans1:17).

Surrendering then means a person needs to be in right living and relationship if it is to be authentic. When a person is in right relationship with God, the next order is to be in right relationship with others. Then surrendering and casting cares to the Lord is even easier than bass fishing.

If you were to make a list of daily cares, what would some of them be?

What would be on your list of monumental cares, the ones that burden and overload and are like a shadow that does not go away?

What is so hard about *casting* for you?

Can you practice the act of surrendering by casting on a daily basis?

What do you need to confess and repent of that keeps you from righteous living with God and others?

Jayne Kane

Cast To Me

What are your cares, my child? Talk to me about them . . . . I want you to tell me what they are as a way to communicate with me. My shoulders are big and broad. I am not like earthly fathers who may not have the right motives, the right words or the right knowledge to help you as you cast your cares. My command is that you do not just cast your cares away, but that you cast them onto me. That is the difference between casting and surrendering. When you surrender your cares you are giving them to me to take care of, and you do not need to take them back. This is counterproductive to surrender. As you cast your cares to me, can you feel me sustaining you? Can you feel the load being lifted from your shoulders onto mine? Do you feel lighter? Do you feel freer? This is called being restored and it comes from true surrender. Are you still feeling weighed down and struggling with what righteousness is? If so, tell me what the unrighteousness is? What is wrong in your life? This is what confession and repentance is all about. Talk to me about it . . . . I want you to tell me about your cares as a way to communicate with me. I will not judge or punish you, but I will restore you as you surrender your offenses. I will bring you to righteous living and restoration. David had a desire to have a blameless heart and I know the same can be said for you (Psalm 101:2). I am a God who sustained David and my promises are the same for you and will endure forever. Cast your cares and surrender to me. I will sustain you and will never let you fall.

Surrendering the Vision

Write down the revelation and make it plain on tablets
so that a herald may run with it. For the revelation
awaits an appointed time; it speaks of the end and will
not prove false. Though it lingers, wait for it; it will
certainly come and will not delay.
Habakkuk 2:2-3

Okay, you may be saying "What is this verse all about?" But I want to encourage you to stay with me on this one. This verse was a pivotal passage given to me a long time ago, in December of 1992 during a time with the Lord. It was one of those passages I could not let go of. God was specifically ministering to me that day and it came at a time when I had lost my vision. I was struggling for emotional, physical and spiritual survival. It was such a pivotal ministering time for me that I couldn't leave this passage out of my writing.

I had been praying and reading from The Living Bible, desperately seeking direction from God. Life had reeled out of control and my future was a *black hole*. Being in survival mode, vision was the last thing on my mind. But thankfully, it was foremost in God's mind. As I read from the paraphrase of the Living Bible, Habakkuk 2:2-3 said this "And the Lord said to me, "Write my answer on a billboard large and clear, so that anyone can read it at a glance and rush to tell others. But these things I plan won't happen right away. Slowly, steadily, surely, the time approaches when the vision will be fulfilled. If it seems slow, do not despair, for these things will surely come to pass. Just be patient! They will not be overdue a single day!"

Wow! Those words jumped off the page at me. What did all this mean? All I knew was God was giving me a promise, a reason to go on with hope and encouragement for the future. Somehow, the events that were occurring and the circumstances surrounding the situation were going to be used in the future for something far more than I could imagine at the time. There is something about a person's vision. It is something so built into a person that no matter what happens, it will go away. Vision is as much a part of an individual as the DNA of the person. Vision is about the person's personality, life experiences and what God predestined for that person.

Let's go back to Habakkuk and see what God was saying and revealing here. Habakkuk was a prophet to Israel. The book of Habakkuk is a dialogue between Habakkuk and God. The book is considered to be a private journal, but through God's divine inspiration and intervention, it went public. The book is about Habakkuk's personal struggle with how God operates. He was asking the hard questions about why God allows evil to prevail and win out at times. Where is God in all of this? Why is God's timing not always reasonable? And it addresses the myriad of other questions we as humans do not understand when it comes to God's sovereignty At the time of Habakkuk, the Babylonian's were threatening the Israelites. This was the known end to them. It still comes down to how many times in life do we ask God the same questions Habakkuk was asking?

Habakkuk wanted to see justice prevail. As a prophet, he was given special revelation from God, and yet he was not seeing how the revelation from God and the vision he had for his people were going to line up with what was going on with the Babylonians. That is exactly where I was too, metaphorically anyway. My vision was to one day write a book, a vision I had since I was in the fifth grade. The events of my life at the time, which included loss after loss and my vision were not lining up. The *black hole* of my future just didn't make sense. That was until the December morning of 1992. God told me that slowly my vision would be fulfilled, I didn't fully understand what my vision was, but He did. As God told me to be patient, little did I know He meant I needed to be patient for almost two decades. When He revealed that *these things* would not happen right away, I thought surely it would be in a few weeks or months or at most a few years. But here I am today. The events, circumstances and all that has happened since that December day were not how I planned for life to go. In my wildest dreams I could have never imagined the things that have happened would go the way they have. Not even a best selling novelist could have written my story. But this was the way God wanted to define my vision, not only of writing a book, but of seeing people restored for His purpose.

The main theme of the book or *journal* of Habakkuk could be summarized as this; "Surrendering the vision of restoration of the Israelites to God's plan and sovereignty." In the end Habakkuk says in verses 18 and 19 of chapter 3 "I will rejoice in the Lord, I will be joyful in God my Savior. The Sovereign Lord is my strength; he makes my feet like the feet of a deer, he enables me to go on the heights." Habakkuk's writing became an act of worship to God.

God has given each of us a vision. For many of us, the vision may not be clear or it may be buried. For others, vision seems to have been sidetracked by life circumstances. And unfortunately, for some, there is no perceived or concrete vision, even though God has a plan for everyone. Back in 1992, I had no idea what God was up to. It is only recently that He fully revealed what He has planned for me. Even in that revelation, many details are still a mystery to me. But in surrendering a vision to God there are some promises He gives back through the surrendering;

1. Slowly and in time the vision will be fulfilled.
2. The revelation and accomplishment of the vision will not be one day overdue.
3. God will show up in a big way.

Surrendering a vision means continuing to worship God, no matter what is going on. It means doing the things that will help to bring the vision to revelation. For me it was writing, going back to school, public speaking, becoming a life coach and going through the *crucible of character refinement*. Sometimes surrendering a vision may mean doing nothing at all, just allowing God to do what God will do.

Just this week I talked to a number of people who have visions calling for surrender. Fortunately each person is allowing God to be sovereign and reveal himself and the vision in time. I have a ninety nine year and ten month old physical therapy client whose family abandoned her years ago. She is looking forward to celebrating her one hundredth Birthday. That is her vision. My dear friend needs to have surgery, but before the doctors will do this she has to lose weight. Her vision is to lead a pain free and active life again. That is her vision.

My former boss has been inspired to write a book. That is her vision. A young and broke college graduate whose passion is real estate wants to excel in his field. That is his vision. And yet in each of these visions, the sovereignty of God, His timing, the plan and vision itself has to be surrendered. We don't know the intricacies of what is needed in God's eyes for a vision to be fulfilled.

Habakkuk, in his wisdom and in revelation from God, was able to surrender to God. He knew God is sovereign and God's will and his vision would be accomplished. I can say the same for my vision. In 1992 my vision was a big one, but today as I look ahead, God's vision for me is so much bigger than I imagined back then. I am so glad God knows what He is doing, because I certainly don't. And with that in mind, all of our visions should be surrendered. God's fulfillment of His visions for us will not be overdue a single day!

What is your vision?

Don't have one? Perhaps you may want to see a life purpose coach!

Can you see how the events and circumstances and your personality may be aligning for God to reveal and fulfill your vision?

Why do you think God may be telling you to be patient and to surrender?

What could happen if you take matters in your own hands and jump ahead of God?

Can you worship God as Habakkuk did, surrendering to God because he is sovereign?

My Big Vision

As you dream and ask for revelation for my will and purpose for your life and as you desire to see your vision fulfilled, I ask you to surrender it to me. The poor Israelites lost sight of their vision I planned for them and because they lost their vision, they faltered and failed. My faithful ones, such as Habakkuk were blessed with divine revelation. As he surrendered he worshipped me. Habakkuk was blessed as he understood that I, the Sovereign Lord, was his strength and would take him to new heights (Habakkuk 3:19). Through patience and surrender, you too will see your vision fulfilled. It will not be overdue a single day and surely in time it will come to pass. As you surrender your vision, let Habakkuk be your example. He struggled with my timing and sovereignty, but I allowed his personal struggle and the writing that came from it to be present for all time. Unknowingly, Habakkuk wrote his story to give you hope and encouragement for your own struggle. As I work to refine, grow and reveal my vision for you, surrender it for my glory. Yield your heart to me (Joshua 24:23). Worship me, surrender your vision and purpose to me. Be patient. I have a plan for you that is far greater than you can believe. Take note of that from my prophet, Habakkuk! My plan will not be overdue a single day.

Surrendering in Patience

*Wait for the Lord and keep his way. He will exalt you to
inherit the land; when the wicked are cut off, you will
see it.*
Psalm 37:34

As I sat by the pond in my backyard, I was seeing two of each fish. I
tried to refocus my eyes and thought to myself, "I must be really tired."
But there were still two of each fish. I didn't know what was happening.
I had been under a lot of stress lately and I was overtired. I was alarmed
that two of everything wouldn't go away. As I looked in the mirror I
noticed that my right eye was drooping slightly and was asymmetrical
compared to the left eye. I was worried and anxious, but decided to keep
the concern to myself. The next day I made an eye doctor appointment.
The gentlemanly optometrist who I had been a patient of nearly my
entire life tried not to show his own concern, but I could tell he was
alarmed. He referred me to an ophthalmologist on an emergency basis.
My mind was racing. I was entering a state of numbness. Everything
seemed surreal. I thought, "This can't be happening." I didn't have
time for this! The ophthalmologist was concerned that I might have
myasthenia gravis. He had already ruled out multiple sclerosis. None of
this was good, no matter what it would turn out to be. An emergency
MRI was scheduled but it would be a few days before the results would
be read. Tick tock, tick tock the clock went.

My double vision didn't change. But instead I began experiencing
numbness and tingling on the right side of my face. I found myself not
being able to say my "S's" quite as clearly and I felt like I was drooling, but
I wasn't. I couldn't sleep and I couldn't tell anyone except my husband.
My prayer was "Please God, please God, take this away!" Finally the
doctor called. It appeared that I had a benign meningeoma at the base
of my skull in the brain stem. He asked me to see a neurosurgeon on

an emergency basis the same afternoon. So my husband and I dropped everything and away we went. As I sat in the doctor's office, I had a sick feeling in my stomach. Tick tock, tick tock the clock went.

Finally, at 5:30 we were called to the exam room. As the neurosurgeon looked at the pictures of my brain, he muttered, "We will have to do exploratory surgery. You may not survive the surgery and we will have to first do an angiogram and some other tests to see if it is feasible to even do such a thing. You will probably be paralyzed on your right side as the tumor is in a difficult spot and it's not reasonable to think that there won't be brain damage. Come back next week and we will proceed. In the meantime, go home and do the best you can." Tick tock, tick tock.

How would I tell my seventeen and eighteen year-old sons? How could I function? What did the future hold? I didn't have time for this and I didn't have the strength to be patient. Life as I knew it was about to change. Events continued to happen. Three different people who didn't know each other called and suggested I go to Mayo Clinic in Rochester. I called my ophthalmologist and told him my desire. He wouldn't give me a referral as he didn't know any doctors there. I simply told him that I was going to Mayo Clinic with or without his blessing, but that a letter of referral would expedite things. Reluctantly he agreed to write the referral letter for me and away we went. Tick tock, tick tock.

I had a team of doctors at Mayo. There was not a whole lot to look at other than my eye, face and the MRI scans. My neurosurgeon was an approachable and kind man. As he silently examined the MRI scan he was deep in thought. Tick tock, tick tock. Finally he said, "It appears to be as the radiologist diagnosed: a benign meningioma. There is no way to know for sure though. I would like you to go home and then in two months I want to do another MRI and see how it is growing." When I asked about surgery or at least a biopsy he smiled and kindly said, "The best brain surgeon in the world would never be able to get that brain tumor out of you." After he left the exam room I looked at the array of certificates on his wall and to my amazement, discovered that *he was* one of the best brain surgeons in the world! So we went home. Tick tock, tick tock.

Two months later it was confirmed I did indeed have a benign meningeoma and was definitely inoperable. But what was the next step?

The following appointments were about trying radiation. I would lose my hair, but not my life. Radiation would not paralyze me, but quite possibly it would not be effective either. And they would be doing it over the Christmas holiday season, because the sooner the better. Tick tock, tick tock.

I was on a rollercoaster. I just wanted to be normal again. I wanted to spend the holiday with my husband and sons and I wanted to go back to work. I wanted the double vision and the headaches I was having from being *cross-eyed* to be gone. I was weary from not being able to focus my eyes and I just wanted the numbness in my face to go away. As we rode the elevator out of the building at the Mayo clinic my cell phone rang. The neurosurgeon was calling with one other alternative. He was going to have a neuroradio surgeon call me. Tick tock, tick tock.

The neuroradio surgeon consulted with my brain surgeon and together they determined I was a candidate for gamma knife surgery. It would be surgery without a knife, using gamma rays to destroy the DNA that would make the tumor grow. The primary goal of the surgery was to stabilize the tumor and keep it from growing any bigger. At the time of the surgery, the hope was that the tumor would shrink just enough to take the pressure off the optic nerve to alleviate the double vision. But time would tell. In the meantime, I was advised to go back to living a *normal* life as best as I could. Tick tock, tick tock.

Today the meningeoma has shrunk by up to fifty percent. My doctor can not explain why, but just simply says "There appears to be no adverse affect to the nerves and surrounding tissue from the tumor itself or the gamma knife surgery." I would like to say that I did a good and godly job of surrendering the situation in the weeks and months I was going through this ordeal. But I didn't. I was angry at God. I was demanding and impatient. I screamed and yelled and cried. I didn't surrender in patience and yet God was faithful. The years following were filled with far more difficult circumstances than I experienced during those four months. The brain tumor was a trial that prepared me for a deeper level of surrender to patience.

Wait for the Lord. Surrender in patience. Keep His way. That means living a life that would radiate the love of God. Live the life of a lily! God will exalt you. He will lift you above your circumstances. If only I had surrendered in patience that fall I would have enjoyed my son's football games more. I would have loved being home in the gorgeous autumn weather we had that year. I would have laughed at the two kittens friends had given us. I would have enjoyed the apples I picked, even though I was seeing two of them at all times! If I had surrendered in patience, I would have been a more pleasant person to be around and the whole ordeal would have been kept in perspective.

Surrender in patience. I was given an extra measure of grace during this time. Hundreds of people who did not even know me, prayed for me on their prayer chains. I was spared. I was healed! But it was not a result of surrendered patience. Tick tock, tick tock. The choice is to be patient and surrender or to rebel against what is happening. Waiting for the Lord and keeping his way means living life as God intended in spite of all that is happening.

As the clock goes tick, tock, tick, tock, what are you surrendering or not surrendering?

Can you draw from a past experience to help you have perspective in the current circumstance?

Is there another Bible passage that helps you to surrender in patience?

As you surrender in patience, what things can you do to enhance the time?

When you surrender in patience it means seeing a life circumstance as an opportunity or an obstacle. Which one are you surrendering to?

My Patience

    David wrote the beloved Psalm 37 and through those words he ministered to those who are waiting in surrender. He was bringing a message of hope. Hope in me as you struggle with being patient. David knew that I am a God of provision and that is how he was able to say I would exalt him to inherit the land. My clock does not go tick tock, but rather it says "Trust, trust in me with patience." I want to give you a secure entitlement of inheritance, but not so much physically as spiritually. Of course I want you to experience the riches of the Promised Land, but the real Promised Land will be when you are with me in eternity. Surrender in patience, as I am also being patient as I prepare the land for you. As you surrender and are patient, see obstacles as opportunities and trust that I am your God of provision. When you are in surrendered patience, trust and hope can bloom. My process of restoration and healing can be expedited. And people will see me through you. Do not doubt me in your heart (Mark 11:23). There are blessings in surrendering in patience. I promise you will be exalted.

Surrendered Servant Hood

*After that he (Jesus) poured water into a basin and
began to wash his disciples' feet, drying them with the
towel that was wrapped around him.*
John 13:5.

This story took place just before Jesus entered Jerusalem during
the last week of His life leading to the culmination of events on the
cross. John is the only one who recorded the foot washing event. It is
one of the most powerful examples of humble servant hood to ever be
recorded. Let's set the stage for this. Jesus and His disciples had been
in ministry together for nearly three years. Much of the time Jesus
spent His energy on equipping His disciples for the time when they
would do ministry without Him. But even at this point in the story,
the disciples argued over who Jesus' favorite might be (See Luke 22).
On this evening they were all eating supper together, which would
later be recounted as *The Last Supper.* This was the last time all twelve
disciples were together. Even Judas Iscariot, who would betray Jesus
shortly, was with them. The meal was possibly the Passover Feast, so
it was not just an ordinary time of fellowship and eating. Normally,
the foot washing was done by a servant before the meal. But Jesus
deliberately took the role of servant during the meal to make a point.
As we read the whole story we can see it must have been unnerving
for the disciples. Peter even commented on what Jesus was doing. As
Jesus finishes, He reveals the lesson to be learned is one of true servant
hood. He ends the evening by telling the disciples that since they now
knew the things He had taught them about servant hood, they would
be blessed if they *did* them.

Everything from Jesus washing all twelve of the disciples' feet
(including Judas Iscariot's) to using the towel wrapped around His waist
was a graphic example of surrendering to servant hood. Jesus did not

cut corners. He did not just talk about servant hood and He did not wash just a few of the disciples' feet. He did it in complete humility and without complaining or fanfare. He could have washed the disciples' feet in public and created a scene. But He did it specifically for the people He was training to follow with servant hearts. Jesus served with a humbled heart, the core of surrendered servant hood.

We are all faced on a daily basis with opportunities to practice servant hood. Almost every interaction with another human can be considered servant hood. But the big question is, "Is the servant hood done with a surrendered heart? Is there patience, humility and pure and a true motive for serving?" As I thought about this story, many of my own stories of how I have been called to servant hood came to mind. But I haven't always served with a surrendered heart. Ironically, I have been more blessed by the people I served than I was a blessing to those I served.

Over the years, my physical therapy patients (too many to count) have blessed me. My sons, who as a mother I have been called to serve, have blessed me, despite my shortcomings and failings. My friends who I sometimes don't call often enough, continue to bless me. And when I have a coaching client, I know ahead of time I will be more blessed than how I bless them.

One of my earliest memories of surrendered servant hood came at the age of sixteen. I wanted to get into physical therapy school. My underlying motive for becoming a nursing assistant was that it would look good on the application for physical therapy school. I started working at a nursing home in a nearby town. I had the experience of a life time! The nursing home was in an old brick building that had been converted from an old hospital. It was dark, dingy and there was no air conditioning. In the heat of the summer, it was like a brick oven. Many of the residents were completely disabled and some were physically and verbally abusive because of cognition problems. There were four of us working the evening shift, entirely responsible for forty residents. In my naivety I had no idea what I was getting myself into. But during the two years I worked there, I learned invaluable lessons from the nurse who took me under her wing and taught me about compassion. I learned from my co-workers what it meant to take care of each other. And I learned from the residents.

One of these residents was Tillie. She had a front tooth missing, was a little scary looking and was completely wheelchair bound. She had no family to speak of. She had a mean streak in her and when angry, would swing at the staff, even when they were trying to help her. But on several occasions, as I tucked her into bed at night she would give me a hug. Even today yet, I can envision that old nursing home, the smells and the people who called it home. For me it was my first lesson in surrendered servant hood. Initially, my motive for serving there was to put it on my resume and application for school. But in the end it was an experience that shaped me for life. It was a real life lesson in surrendered servant hood.

What opportunities in your life have had you take off your cloak, get on the floor and wash another's feet?

What is the difference between servant hood and surrendered servant hood?

Do you serve with ulterior motives or with the motives Jesus served?

How will you change your attitude, motive or perspective to align your surrendered servant hood with the servant hood of Jesus?

Surrendering the Towel

I have equipped you with opportunities, gifts and all you need to serve others. And in many cases I can say to you "Well done, good and faithful servant." But now I am asking you to go to a new level with your serving. Surrender the towel you keep with you to protect and insulate yourself. Much attention has been paid to who I served as I washed twenty four feet. But I ask you to focus on the towel I used. I wrapped it around myself, but then I used it to dry those feet. I exposed myself to help the ones I was called to serve. I surrendered what I had protecting me to serve my disciples. As you learn and practice surrendered servant hood, I ask you to use all that I have given you. Look to me with a servant heart (Psalm 123:2). Use your surrendered servant hood to love others. You may be surprised as to whom you will be called to serve, but as I promised the disciples, you will be blessed. Take off your towel and surrender your servant hood. In doing so you will show me how deep your own love is for me.

A Surrendered Family

"Martha, Martha," the Lord answered, you are worried
and upset about many things, but only one thing is
needed. Mary has chosen what is better, and it will not
be taken away from her."
Luke 10:41-42

This is a classic Bible story containing many valuable lessons. It portrays a picture of Martha, busy with needless things and Mary being the one to *be with* Jesus. I can just picture the scene. Jesus shows up in Bethany at the home of Mary and Martha. Keep in mind there was no phone or communication system available to give the house of Mary and Martha notice that Jesus was coming. So Jesus shows up unexpectedly. My guess is Martha is the older of the two sisters and was the responsible one. It was part of her personality and her role in the birth order to be the one to put it all together. Interestingly, in verse 38 Martha is given credit for opening her home to Jesus. So here we have two sisters who appear to be quite different from one other. Martha complains to her guest, Jesus, and He tells her that Mary, who is *just sitting around* is complimented while Martha is corrected!

This presents interesting dynamics. Does it sound familiar for your family? Do you have family members whose personalities are different from each other? Or if you have a small family or perhaps no family to speak of, what about your other relationships, which then become your family? And then we have the church family and all the dynamics that go along with it. I am no expert on family dynamics, but I am a part of a family. I experience all the dynamics that goes along with it. And it really is no different than the Mary/ Martha House of Bethany, Palestine in about 30 A.D.

What happens in a family when something unexpected happens? Let's say Jesus shows up unexpectedly at your house and needs a place to stay. Inadvertently someone would shove things into a closet, make a quick grocery list, and clear a space on the couch for Jesus to sit down. Probably someone in the family would be unaffected by the unexpected guest and would be able to just *be*. Are there unspoken rules about who does what in your? Are there silent expectations about the roles in your family? Who and what determines the family roles and rules? I suspect nearly every family faces this dilemma at some point.

Some years back I was criticized for not taking the role of chief communicator in my extended family. Both my parents had died and the natural chain of communication had been broken. Events such as births, deaths, illnesses and the likes were not going through a chain of communication. I had no idea this role was my responsibility, since I am the oldest child in my family. Apparently there were some who assumed I would fill the role of chief communicator. I offended some people who thought I was withholding information intentionally. It was not the case at all. I just thought everyone talked to everyone else and information was communicated by whoever picked up the phone.

This is the types of situation where all I can do is to throw my hands up and say to God, "I am surrendering this to you, and I am just going to be!" Families, both immediate and extended can be complex and entangled. Over the years I learned to not judge, analyze or try to figure out family dynamics. Most often, as I discovered, surrendering each member in prayer and just *being* in the presence of Jesus has been the best approach. Interestingly, I have then been asked "Don't you care?"

Being surrendered in a family does not mean that caring stops. It just means the emotional hook that trapping a person is not a factor in the relationship. There are psychological terms and clinical methods for dealing with family dynamics. But I want to focus on what Jesus was saying instead. He brought the priorities of Mary and Martha into perspective. He commended Mary for just *being*. He was concerned for Martha and her busyness, which was fueled by her anxiety. Jesus had insight into Martha's motives and this was what He was most concerned about. It wasn't that Jesus didn't want her to entertain and be a good host, nor did He want her to lose her focus and priorities. Jesus wanted her to have the same perspective that Mary did. He wanted Martha to be as surrendered as Mary was.

At times there is nothing more difficult than living life as a family. When a family is operating surrendered to Jesus, there is no bigger blessing. When each family member surrenders their motives, perspectives, focus, roles, rules and expectations to Jesus, then room is made for *being*. *Being* is a state of surrender with a central focus on what is most important. It is a state of surrender where anxiety, worry, fear, anger, bitterness, unforgiveness and discouragement have been erased. *Being* a family means surrendering the dynamics and allowing the presence of Jesus to permeate the heart of the family, one by one. If Jesus paid a visit to my house, I'm not sure if I would be the one to run around, cleaning the place up or if I would sit down at His feet and *be* with Him. I guess the answer is, it depends on how messy the house is and if I had been grocery shopping lately!

As a member of a family (whether it is your birth family or church or other type of family) what role do you usually take?

When you are faced with dynamics, how do you react?

If Jesus knocked on the door at your home what would you do?

What parts or members of your *family* do you need to intentionally surrender to God?

As you surrender family members and dynamics, what are you telling yourself?

Jayne Kane

My Visit to You

    As I knock on the door of your home, I want you to know that I do not care about what condition it is in. I am coming to be with you and I only ask that you be with me. Surrender all the worry and anxiety that comes with the cares of daily life. And while you are surrendering to me, surrender your family to me too. Release yourself of the entanglement that comes with the relational aspects of being a part of a family. Continue to intercede for one another and check your own motives and perspective. Surrender the roles and rules of your family to me and come into my presence. Ask for the Holy Spirit to permeate your family so love may abound and grow in each member. Learn to live in forgiveness and with an attitude of surrender. And keep the focus on me. As I come into your home, live as though I am physically, not just spiritually there. Live in a state of being, the state of complete surrender bringing peace and love to the heart. As the heart of your family is opened to my presence, love me and love each other with all your heart, soul and mind (Matthew 22:37). There are Mary and Martha's in every family. And there are dynamics and emotional entanglements in every family. Surrender and being will erase those entanglements and will allow my Spirit to work in ways where you will be immeasurably blessed.

Shake the Dust Off in Surrender

If anyone will not welcome you or listen to your words,
shake the dust off your feet when you leave that home or
town.
Matthew 10:14

Jesus was giving direction to the disciples in an orientation session before going out into the ministry field. And this verse in Matthew was one of the principles Jesus had for His twelve handpicked disciples. Jesus was teaching the disciples on how to set boundaries and when to surrender a situation and walk away. Jesus knew firsthand that His disciples would not be popular everywhere they went. He knew there would be times when they would need to walk away or they would be emotionally, spiritually and maybe even physically destroyed. The disciples' purpose as they went from town to town would be to carry the message of who Jesus was and what He was all about. They would go to towns where there would be Israelites as well as Gentiles. And there were always the Pharisees and the Roman rulers to make matters even more complicated.

As they got their instructions from Jesus, He told them there would be times when they would not be welcomed or when the message they carried would be rejected. Jesus' answer to this was to shake the dust off their feet and walk away. Shaking the dust off the feet was a ceremonial act the Pharisees did when leaving an *unclean* Gentile area. It was a symbolic act of rejection. But it was also a way for the disciples to surrender and they realized there would be times when they could do nothing more than walk away and surrender the person or people to God's sovereignty.

Personally, I like the idea of shaking the dust off my feet. Sometimes I wear my sandals when I go for a walk on the gravel road that goes past my house. The dust clings to my feet and sandals making it difficult to just shake the dust off. I take the garden hose and spray the dust off my feet. I would have to say that surrendering situations which are not healthy or godly can be difficult too. Nevertheless, Jesus gives us the same command He gave to the disciples.

How does a person know when to walk away in surrender or when to stay to try to make a difference? There's no real recipe or formula, but there are some guidelines to help with the discernment process. First and foremost, asking the Holy Spirit to guide and direct is the way to discern the will of God. The disciples had the power of the Holy Spirit after Jesus left them. When they began their ministry with Jesus they had Him to personally guide them. Secondly, the Ten Commandments need to be followed and adhered to. The best part is that we have the power of God's written Word to give us further direction and provide instruction to know when a situation must be surrendered.

I had to walk away from a number of situations and circumstances over the years. It was hard not to look back and at the time I wasn't sure if I was doing the right thing by surrendering. But in time, it became clear it was the right and godly thing to do. And always, God blessed me for following His instructions.

In my younger years there were people who were not a godly influence whom I chose not to spend my time with. At the time I was criticized and teased for my choice. There were work situations where I prayed my way through for God to give me strength to walk. These environments were corrupt and unhealthy, sapping me emotionally, spiritually and physically. God honored my desire to live a Godly life and I was able to walk away, shake the dust from my feet and surrender to His plan for me. There have been situations in the community of faith too, where I could do nothing (after trying everything) surrendering the church to God. There have been other times over the years where I had to make choices based on what would be spiritually and emotionally healthy for me.

Even Jesus faced a time when He had to walk away and shake the dust from his feet. Luke records such an episode in chapter 4. Jesus had been baptized and filled with the Holy Spirit. It was early in His ministry and was going around Galilee teaching in the synagogues. He went back to Nazareth where He grew up and revealed to the people there that He was the one who the prophet Isaiah had talked about hundreds of years earlier. They still thought of Him as Joseph's son and could not fathom the idea of Jesus being the Messiah. They took after Him with a plan to throw Him over a cliff. But here is the best part, Jesus walked right through the rioters and walked away.

That is what happens when you surrender and shake the dust off and walk away. God's divine power of protection and provision takes over. Even Jesus had times when all He could do was walk away. Sadly He had to walk away from the people who had seen Him grow up. Jesus understood how it felt to surrender when something was not right. The unshakable love of God and the power of the Holy Spirit made things right.

Did you ever have to shake the dust from your feet and walk away from something or someone?

If you have not had to, is there a time and place now where you need to shake the dust off your feet in surrender?

Was or is it for your good or the other person's good?

Did you use the power and godly principles of the Ten Commandments, the Holy Spirit and the Bible?

When you look back, can you see how surrender was the right and godly thing to do?

What situation or person do you see from the past where you should have walked away from and surrendered?

How did God use that to teach and refine you?

Jayne Kane

Dusty Feet

As you travel the road of life and pick up dust from the roads, allow me to instruct you on when to surrender. In those times and circumstances when you are rejected for your godly beliefs, when you stand up for me and when you are criticized for your faith in me, allow me to guide you on the ways to surrender. Sometimes surrender is a way of releasing to me what only I can take care of. Sometimes surrender is a way of allowing me to protect you. As I instructed my disciples and told them about wolves dressed in sheeps' clothing, I also told them when to shake the dust from their feet and walk away. I told them to not only walk away, but to not look back. Even I had to walk away from the town that embraced me as a child, but later rejected the truth of who I really am. Surrender that which is not good and is not good for you. Lean on my commandments, the power of the Holy Spirit and the instructions of the Bible to be your guide. Search me and come to me for guidance on the dusty path. Surrender in the assurance that I am a God of protection. You too will be able to walk through the crowd of rioters as I did when you are on the path of surrender. Shake the dust off your feet and be surrendered. It is my wish and my command for you.

The Ultimate Act of Surrender

Father, into your hands I commit my spirit.
Luke 23:42

It is finished.
John 19:30

In closing this time of surrender, what it is and what it can do, the realization I came to is there is one single episode recorded in Scripture which supersedes all other acts or examples of surrender. As I studied and prayed about this revelation, it brought me to my knees. I had never seen the life and death of Jesus in this way before. And even as I write this, I am confessing and repenting of my own callousness to what Jesus did as the ultimate act of surrender.

By now, you may have recorded your own times of surrender and it is my hope and prayer you gained a deeper understanding of what surrender is all about. As you laugh and cry about living or not living a surrendered life, it is my vision for you to find restoration as you surrendered. Surrender is the only way to true healing and restoration for this time on earth.

As I sat on the front porch on this last summer evening, there was a hint of fall in the air. The sunset had the look of autumn in it as oranges and yellows blended together. It is late summer and the birds are banding together. The bluebirds had grown up and were swinging from the utility line as they planned for a trip south. A flock of red wing black birds swarmed to the near by tall grass. Even the Canadian geese are a little restless as they fly overhead. As I watched the comical hummingbirds fight over the birdfeeder as they plump up for their trip south, I thought about *seasons*. Seasons come and go here in the Midwest. We have four definite seasons, each one with its blessings and challenges. As hearty Minnesotans we have a choice when it comes to the seasons. We can embrace and surrender to them or we can complain and fight them. I would like to think most of us try to embrace and surrender to the challenge of each season.

Life itself is much the same way. Quite often I think about a time when I had to surrender and the end result left me grieving and asking God a lot of questions as I tried to learn a lesson on surrender. Shortly after the fall of Communism in the Eastern European nations in the late 1980 and early 1990's adoptions from those countries became possible. My husband felt a tug at his heart as we learned about the orphanages in those countries filled with children in need of homes. He got the idea that we should adopt a Romanian orphan. I prayed about my husband's desire, not totally convinced we should adopt. After all, we had two children and my life was chaotic enough. I surrendered to God's plan and we began the adoption process. Everything moved along, the home study was complete, the money was paid and they located a little eighteen month-old girl from an orphanage in Pitesti, Romania for us. She had an older sister who had been adopted in California. I got her room ready and every day I looked at her picture wondering what it would be like to have a little girl. Finally the court proceedings were complete in Bucharest. The plan was for my husband to go to Romania to get her and I would stay home with our sons. We were a week away from going to get her, and then . . . .

Romania closed the door to American adoptions. The Romanian government had been told Americans were buying their babies. Their answer to this was to immediately ban American adoptions. Our caseworker in Romania tried for several months to advocate for us. Hundreds of people prayed for our little girl and our family. But it did not happen. Eventually we knew adopting our little girl wasn't going to happen. We knew we could no longer fight to get her. I grieved and surrendered her to the Lord's care. I hope to meet her and hold her in heaven some day. It was so difficult to surrender her and to let go. To think of how God had to surrender His son, Jesus, is beyond comprehension when I think about surrendering my own child. God surrendered His son to a death. We only surrendered our daughter to the Romanian government.

We can embrace whatever season we are in or we can fight it. And Jesus, as a human, earthly man, experienced the same. The season at the end of His ministry was not a season He looked forward to. In fact

He asked God to take the time and trial away from Him. But God did not. As Jesus hung on the cross, bleeding and dying a slow death, He called out to God, "My God, my God, why have you forsaken me?" But then very close to the end, He said to God, "Father into your hands I commit my Spirit." And then finally He said, "It is finished." *This* was the ultimate act of surrender.

Father God must have anguished even more than we did when we lost our daughter. Jesus surrendered His life, His suffering and His death to God His Father. As He hung on that wooden cross dying a horrible death, He was able to surrender to God's will and purpose for His life.

He did it for me. And He did it for you.

If Jesus would do that for me, then what am I doing for Him?

Recently I was seeing an elderly ninety three year-old gentleman for physical therapy in his home. He told me he was an alcoholic and had been drunk for the first half of his life. The second half of his life he practiced sobriety and had helped others with theirs. He talked of his faith and how his belief in God had helped him. Just before I left this man's apartment, a small simple sketch that hung on his kitchen wall caught my eye. This is what it said:

I asked Jesus
"How much do you love me?"
"This much,"
He answered, and He
stretched out His arms and died.

It brought me to tears. It was so simple and yet profound. It brought into perspective just what surrender is. I asked my client where he had gotten the sketch, but he could not remember. It had hung in his kitchen for so long that he could not remember where it came from. I could not stop thinking about that sketch. I had never seen Jesus hanging on the cross, from the perspective of having His arms out stretched for me in total surrender to whatever came to Him, even death with Him saying to me "This is how much I love you."

In return, living a surrendered life for Jesus seems like such a small thing after seeing what He surrendered to. What if He hadn't gone through that season of surrender? What if He was no longer divine in nature and acted only as a human? What if we did not have a God of restoration? All that we do here on this earth would be a total waste.

Living a surrendered life is not easy. But it is the closest thing to living as Jesus lived. As He stretched out His arms on the cross for you and for me, can you hear Him saying "I love you this much"? I can.

There was an opportunity in the section on simplicity for you to accept Jesus as your Savior. You may not have been ready answer the questions at that time, but perhaps you are now.

Have you surrendered your life to God, acknowledging He sent Jesus, His son to die for you and me?

Do you believe this?

If you do, are you willing to confess and repent of your sins in exchange for Jesus surrendering His life for you?

If this is the first time you have answered these questions and would like to have someone pray with you, I would encourage you to find a believer in Jesus to help you. Living a surrendered life with Jesus and for Him is the only way of having a life and heart that is truly restored not for just our time on this earth but for all of eternity.

My Open Arms

In this season of your life I am with you. I have always been with you and always will be. But at this moment in this season, I ask that you open not only your arms to meet my open arms, but that you will also open your heart to me. As you open your arms and heart, surrender your life to me, your Lord and Savior. I love you more than any earthly human ever could. And this is the only reason I would ask you to surrender totally to me. Come into my arms and know that I will protect you and provide for you. As I hung on the cross for that brief time and then was brought to glory through resurrection, I want you to experience the benefits of that brief time. I desire for you to be restored and to one day also be resurrected to spend eternity with me (Psalm 51:12). Believe in me and believe this. Come to me and rest in my arms. As you go into a new season of restoration, live a surrendered life that others will take notice of. As they see you restored and surrendered you will be living the way you were created to be. Open your arms to me. My arms are open to you. I love you and am waiting for you to surrender and have your heart be all mine.

Final Thoughts on Surrender

Surrender at any level can be difficult. Admittedly there are times in life when surrender is easier than other times. Practicing a life of surrender is something that needs to be done on a daily basis. In our human state and under our own power surrendering is nearly impossible. As humans we desire to take control and have power over our lives. This desire for control keeps us from surrendering. Thinking we have power and control is a lie and is like living in a cloud. The truth is there is very little we can actually control in life. The key to surrender is prayer and relying on the power of the Holy Spirit. So live with a heart restored to how God intended it. Live with passion, love and with a peace that comes when Jesus is in the center of your surrender.

From this section on surrender—
Surrender in prayer all that you have and all that you struggle with.
Surrender to God the strongholds that keep you bound and from living a restored life.
Surrender your relationship with God to Him.
Surrender so God can equip you for His glory.
Surrender with Abraham-like faith.
Surrender to God in righteousness.
Surrender all your cares to God.
Surrender your vision, plans and purpose to God.
Surrender in patience.
Surrender your servant hood to God.
Surrender your family to God.
Surrender to God what is not good for you.
Surrender your life to God and all of you to Jesus!

Conclusion

I hope that you have grown, laughed, cried, shouted "amen!" prayed, journaled (even just a little) and learned as you read these reflections. The journey of restoration is unique for each person and there is no timeline as to how long or what the journey will be like. Keep in mind, restoration goes on for a lifetime. It will only be when we are in heaven with Jesus when we will ultimately be restored. But it doesn't mean we cannot enjoy living a life abundantly restored for this time on earth.

I shared with you my own journey of restoration so you would be encouraged. Perhaps you were able to relate to parts of my story, or maybe you gained a new perspective as you read how I struggled and groaned through the process. Have I *arrived*? No. Not entirely. Remember how I compared healing to that of the layers of an onion? The thing is that just when I think there is nothing more to be uncovered, something comes along to humble me, expose me and put me on my knees to God again. It took me years to be able to share how God has used all the parts of my life to bring hope and encouragement to others. I am so humbled to have been given the opportunity to share this with you.

As you continue to rely on the Holy Spirit and His Word for Truth, I hope you will discover far more than what is in this book. The Bible is full of stories of restoration. There are many examples in it in which you can personally relate to the stories and characters as you continue to read, study and pray.

As you continue your journey of restoration, claim Bible verses, chapters and biblical characters for yourself. You will want to be able to come back to these helps in a heartbeat. Mark the parts in your Bible that *jump* off the page with which you identify most closely. If you are not connected with other believers in Jesus as Savior, I would encourage you to seek those people out. Iron sharpens iron and this is what doing life as believers in Christ is all about. If you still need to work through the questions you left unanswered or linger in you mind, seek out a trusted clergy person or mentor. And finally, if you find that you need to take steps in moving further along in your journey of restoration, consider meeting with a Christian life coach.

There is a part of me that doesn't want this book to be finished. It has been a lifelong dream of mine to write a book such as this and I am asking myself "What next?" But at the same time I am excited about the opportunities God will give me to see others bloom and live as restored people—his design for all of us. Finally I want to share a common comment I hear from people. It is "I would like to write a book". Each of us has a book within ourselves and I encourage you to share your own story and journey with others. Sharing in itself is healing and restorative!

I love a favorite old hymn describing the journey of restoration we all are on. The melody is as beautiful as the words. As you read this hymn, let the words permeate your heart and mind. It is a song of assurance, trust and the words bring hope and encouragement which are true for all time.

When peace, like a river, attendeth my way,
When sorrows like sea billows roll—
Whatever my lot, Thou hast taught me to say.
It is well; it is well with my soul, with my soul
It is well; it is well with my soul.

Tho Satan should buffet, tho trials should come,
Let this blest assurance control,
That Christ hath regarded my helpless estate,
And has shed his own blood for my soul.
It is well; it is well with my soul, with my soul
It is well; it is well with my soul.

My sin—O the bliss of this glorious thought
My sin, not in part, but the whole,
Is nailed to the cross, and I bear it no more:
Praise the Lord, praise the Lord, O my soul!

It is well; it is well with my soul, with my soul
It is well; it is well with my soul.

And, Lord, haste the day when my faith shall be sight,
The clouds be rolled back as a scroll:
The trump shall resound and the Lord shall descend,
"Even so"—it is well with my soul.
It is well; it is well with my soul, with my soul
It is well; it is well with my soul.

By Horatio G. Stafford
1828-1888
Public Domain

Be Encouraged in Love and Hope,

Jayne